Dance

To William, Casper and Oscar, and all the dancers
and choreographers who have inspired me – A.S.

To Jen, whose feedback and critiques
are often hard to swallow but usually right – J.R.

BIG PICTURE PRESS

First published in the UK in 2023 by Big Picture Press,
an imprint of Bonnier Books UK,
4th Floor, Victoria House
Bloomsbury Square, London WC1B 4DA
Owned by Bonnier Books
Sveavägen 56, Stockholm, Sweden
www.bonnierbooks.co.uk

Design copyright © 2023 by Big Picture Press
Illustration copyright © 2023 by Jason Raish
Text copyright © 2023 Sir Alistair Spalding

1 3 5 7 9 10 8 6 4 2

ISBN 978-1-80078-336-2

This book was typeset in Gill Sans and Neima.
The illustrations were created digitally by building up layers of pencil and paint with a tablet.

The cover design is based on a photograph of Hu Shenyuan from the dance duet Samsara, kindly supplied by Tom Duffin.

Creative Team
Editors Joanna McInerney and Victoria Garrard
Designers Olivia Cook, Winsome d'Abreu and Dave Brown at APE Ltd
Production Controller Neil Randles
Consultants Sojirat Singholka, Pichet Klunchun, Dr Alan Cummings,
Jonzi D, Alesandra Seutin and The Officers of the Morris Ring

Printed in China

This book was produced in association with Sadler's Wells Theatre.
Sadler's Wells is a world leader in contemporary dance, presenting a vibrant year-round programme
of dance of every kind – from tango to hip hop, ballet to flamenco, Bollywood to cutting-edge contemporary
dance – bringing the best of international and British dance to audiences at their three theatres in London.

With special thanks to William Forsythe, Russell Maliphant, Darcey Bussell, Carlos Acosta, Akram Khan and Sir Matthew Bourne.

Welcome to the Arts
ADMIT ALL

Dance

Written by **Sir Alistair Spalding**

Illustrated by **Jason Raish**

BPP

Preface

If you play music for a small toddler, they will almost absolutely start to dance: they will spin, jump, wiggle and sway. These basic movements are a part of every dance style in the world, and the fundamental lexicon for both the professional and amateur dancer.

Dancing is part of being human. Whether to the beat of a drum or a disco tune, it is in our deepest nature to want to move our bodies to a rhythm. As a child, this instinct is clear as soon as we can walk (or even before!). Some of us go on to train professionally and perfect our dancing skills, showing them off on stage. Others find joy through dance recreationally or as part of a ceremony or tradition that brings community together.

This book will explore some of the many ways that we can dance. There are as many different dance styles as there are countries in the world, from flamenco to hip hop, ballet to Balinese legong. Although all of these styles are very different and could separate us, they in fact bring us together in a common humanity. In our interconnected world, dance is available to everyone, be it at our local dance studio or community centre. It is a visual language, understood by all, no matter where you come from.

This book is a journey through this wonderful world of human movement. So, put on your dancing shoes and join us!

Sir Alistair Spalding CBE
Artistic Director & Chief Executive
of Sadler's Wells Theatre, London

THIS WAY PLEASE

Welcome to
Dance

You are cordially invited to an evening of live entertainment unlike anything you have seen before. Featuring the very best performances from around the world from *Swan Lake* to *Riverdance*, you will also rub shoulders with legendary choreographers and performers of both the past and present, including Antonio Gades, Rudolf Nureyev and Pina Bausch. Exclusive backstage access allows you to see what goes on behind the theatre doors, including prop and costume design, which you can admire in magnificent detail.

Brilliantly curated and beautifully illustrated, Welcome to the Arts offers an all-hours admission to some of the world's most wondrous performances.

Get ready to shimmy, sway and dance the night away. Take a seat. The show is about to begin...

The Art of Making a Dance

'*Dancers are instruments, like a piano the choreographer plays.*' So said the great choreographer George Balanchine (1904–1983). But what is a choreographer, and how do they create the routines that dancers perform?

It is often said that dance is ephemeral – that it only exists in the moment and disappears. But it is also true that a theatre dance doesn't exist at all before the act of choreography starts. When a choreographer walks into the studio on the first day of rehearsal for a new production, nothing at all exists, but six weeks later a dance has been created! The dancers are the clay from which the choreographer sculpts the movement.

How do they start? Many choreographers, like Balanchine or New York-based choreographer Mark Morris (born 1956), begin with a piece of music. They study the score (the written form of the music) first, and create a movement that responds to its energy. Others, such as Sir Matthew Bourne (see pages 48–49), want to create a story in dance, and so they begin with movement as a structure that can be followed. Some choreographers, like Trisha Brown (see pages 42–43) or Anne Teresa de Keersmaeker (born 1960), want to express a more abstract idea or emotion.

Choreographers begin to work with the dancers and choose passages of movement that they like and weave it into the piece. Some teach movement sequences by dancing themselves and asking the dancers to copy. For others, it is much more important for the dancers to create movement through improvisation, thus making them co-creators.

There are some basic patterns to follow of course, such as 'unison' where the dancers are performing the same movement at the same time, or 'canon' where a phrase is performed by one group of dancers and then another begins a count later. But essentially, there are no rules in dance, and that is why today there is such a rich variety of styles and approaches. The ultimate aim of a choreographer is to capture both our eye and our emotion.

Now Showing

Rehearsals for *Focus Forsythe: The Choreographer's Process*, 2016 | University of South Carolina Glorya Kaufman School of Dance | Choreography by William Forsythe

American choreographer William Forsythe (born 1949) developed sophisticated improvisation techniques to create the movement in his dances, mainly working with dancers he knew well. In recent years, Forsythe has returned to a purer ballet technique, illustrating the positions he is looking for through demonstration.

Set Design and Lighting

Dance can happen anywhere, and in any setting, but when dance takes to the stage, the elements of lighting and design add another dimension.

Alongside set design, costume, choreography and music, lighting is an important ingredient in any staged dance performance. Aside from the need for the dancers to be well lit, good lighting exaggerates the shapes that the bodies make and highlights facial expressions. But lighting can do much more than simple illumination: it can create atmosphere by capturing a mood, reacting to the colours of the costume to augment, amplify or conceal the dance. In a play, the focus is on dialogue and plot, so the actors' faces are lit using front lighting. Dance, however, is all about movement, so sidelights and backlighting are mostly used to highlight the moving bodies of the dancers.

Most of the time, lighting designers will be involved towards the end of the process and create their designs during technical rehearsals. However, some designers can become co-creators of the work, and begin on day one so that the lighting design is created at the same time as the dance. This can be seen in the work of the award-winning lighting designer Michael Hulls (born 1959), who established a long partnership with the choreographer Russell Maliphant (born 1961).

The remaining design aspects in dance are the costuming (see pages 14–15) and any scenic elements. Physical scenery and painted backdrops have always played a part in set design – from the painted lake in *Swan Lake* (see pages 28–29) through to the soil-covered stage in Pina Bausch's (see pages 46–47) rendering of *The Rite of Spring*. The advent of modern dance saw the removal of traditional scenery and more emphasis placed on lighting. Today, stage design is often achieved through the projection of images on screens. Sophisticated projection technology can transport the audience from a street scene to the interior of a mansion in seconds and without the need for physically heavy sets.

Now Showing

Sylvie Guillem and Russell Maliphant perform in *Push* | Sadler's Wells Theatre, London, 2005
Choreography by Russell Maliphant | Lighting design by Michael Hulls | Music by Andy Cowton

In this piece, Russell Maliphant explored with dancer Sylvie Guillem (born 1965) the possibilities of lifting and releasing, shifting back and forth to support each other's weight. Alongside Maliphant, Guillem and composer Andy Cowton, Michael Hulls became a fourth collaborator, his lighting designs helping to creating the structure of the dance and sculpting the movement.

Costume Design

From dazzling ballroom dresses to romantic tutus, disco flares to embroidered Japanese kimonos, dance costumes can take many different forms. But the key principle for any design is that the dancers need to move!

Dance costuming is a highly specialised field, and many famous designers from Coco Chanel (1883–1971) to Alexander McQueen (1969–2010) have been drawn to its allure. The first (and perhaps most obvious) difference between catwalk designs and costumes is that dancers need to be flexible – having to bend the torso and extend both arms and legs in extreme ways that would never be asked of a model. Fabrics must therefore be durable, stretchy and comfortable.

Aside from the demands of the choreography, the other essential element of costume design is how the costumes portray the concept of the dance to the audience. Colour, texture, and how the fabric moves and interacts with the set design must all be considered to create the perfect effect. The stage lighting must also be considered when costumes are created, as certain pigments and textures can absorb or reflect light, creating different effects – a red

costume under blue lighting will look purple, for example.

Costumes may also have a more traditional design, such as those used in folk or religious dances. Body ornaments and adornments, masks, head pieces, rich patterns and locally sourced materials are used in these ceremonial dances, and often have deep cultural and historical significance. Regardless of the genre, the goals of costuming are the same – to bring the dance to life.

▷——— Now Showing ———◁

1: Oskar Schlemmer designs for *Das Triadisches Ballett* (*The Triadic Ballet*), 1922
Oskar Schlemmer (1888–1943), a Bauhaus painter, sculptor and teacher, created *The Triadic Ballet*. These incredible costumes were not designed for ease of movement. The 'figurines', as Schlemmer called them, informed how the dancers moved. Almost puppet-like, they clattered, bounced and spun around the set, with the dancers merely enlivening the toy characters they had been asked to portray.

2: Alexander McQueen designs for *Eonnagata*, 2009
Based on the extraordinary life of the gender-fluid French diplomat, spy and soldier Chevalier d'Éon (1728–1810), McQueen's designs for *Eonnagata* mix 18th-century French fashion with traditional Japanese styling.

3: Costume worn by a dancer from Adzido Pan African Dance Ensemble, *Sankofa*, 1999
The skirt worn by this dancer is made from a printed textile known as Ankara – a traditional African design printed onto cloth using the Indonesian technique of wax-resist dyeing.

4: Barbara Karinska designs for *Jewels*, 1967
Known for creating iconic costumes for both ballets and Hollywood films, Barbara Karinska (1886–1983) designed the diamond costume for the leading female dancer in the final section of *Jewels* (see pages 34–35). The bodice is liberally embroidered so the performer literally sparkles under the lights.

THEATRE

Ballet

When a ballet dancer enters the room, they stand out. Standing erect and broad-shouldered, they carry themselves with an elegance and deportment that seems to differentiate them from the rest of the us. In fact, ballet dancers are carrying themselves in the same way that French nobles did in the 16th century.

Ballet has a long history, first emerging in the courts of the Italian Renaissance but gaining more importance and profile when it was embraced by the French courts in the 17th century. King Louis XIV (1638–1715), also known as the Sun King, was particularly instrumental in its popularity, and taught ballet to his court to distinguish aristocrats from mere mortals. An impressive ruler (France became the dominant power in Europe during his 72-year reign), the king was also a talented dancer. His first performance was famously as the Sun King in the epic *Ballet Royal de la Nuit,* but he went on to dance in a total of 80 ballets. He also started the first ever dance school in 1661 – the L'Académie Royale de Danse (The Royal Dance Academy).

Ballet became the dance of the French royal court, spreading to other aristocracies across Europe under French political and cultural influence, from Denmark to Russia. Despite the decline of French rule in Europe after the Napoleonic Wars (1803–1815), ballet continued to find root in other European countries, including Germany and Italy. During the early 20th century – after two world wars – ballet found far-reaching popularity in Asia and the Americas.

Today, ballet is the most performed dance style in theatre, and is synonymous with the word 'dance'. It is a thriving art form, and there are ballet companies in every country in the world. It is also the dance style that most children are taught from a young age.

Although the basic ballet technique has remained the same throughout its history, the way that choreographers have used it has continually developed, sometimes moving away from telling stories to more abstract styles where patterns and musical response have replaced narrative (see pages 34–35).

Now Showing

King Louis XIV as the Sun King in *Ballet Royal de la Nuit* | Paris, 1653

Louis became King at the tender age of four during a time of civil war in France. To mark his coming of age and to assert the new monarch's authority, the *Ballet Royal de la Nuit* was created. Split into four parts, the visual spectacle included poetry, music and dance and was performed over 13 hours, from sunset to sunrise. The ballet's defining moment is the rising of the sun: the appearance of the 14-year-old king as Apollo (the Sun King) bringing light and hope to a country in darkness and cementing the notion of the divine right of kings. The king's costume was a lavish cornucopia of gold brocade, ostrich feathers and silks studded with precious stones – a true reflection of the wealth of France at the time.

Ballet Costume

Ballet costumes are an essential part of any performance. With origins deeply associated with aristocracy (see page 19), it is no surprise that ballet dancewear originally used luxurious fabrics and precious stones combined with beautiful designs intended to enhance the visual effects of the movements.

Perhaps the most iconic part of a ballet costume is the pointe shoe – flat, satin or leather slippers with stiff, square toes. Pointe shoes were invented by French dancer and choreographer Charles Didelot (1767–1837) to emphasise the notion of a ballerina being a weightless, ephemeral creature. In 1796, Didelot created a 'flying machine' that not only suspended dancers by wires, but used the first pointe shoe so that the performers could rest on their toes, This 'trick' caught on (without the wire) and the pointe shoe, and associated technique known as pointe work, became a firm fixture of ballet style.

The great French ballet dancer Marie Taglioni (1804–1884), was the first to incorporate pointe work into her performance. Her father, Filippo (1777–1871), was a choreographer and created the role in the ballet *La Sylphide* especially for her. In 1832, Taglioni became the first dancer to wear the romantic tutu. Considered risqué at the time due to its mid-calf length, it was designed to fully reveal Taglioni's pointe skills. Towards the end of the 19th century, as attitudes became more liberal, the length of the tutu gradually shortened with other aspects of the ballet costume becoming more revealing.

The tutu that is most recognised today is known as the modern tutu. It is constructed with layers of tulle (lightweight netting) sewn onto the bodice. The modern tutu allows a much clearer view of the dancer's leg movements and helps to enhance the unison of the *corps de ballet* (a group of dancers).

Now Showing

1: Romantic tutu

This soft, dome-shaped tutu is most recognised in ballets such as *Giselle* and *La Sylphide*. It was designed to enhance the idea of a ballerina as an ethereal creature, not of this world.

2: Classical tutu (pancake)

Worn in performances such as *Swan Lake* and *Don Quixote,* this style is famously seen in Edgar Degas's paintings of scenes at the Paris Opera Ballet.

3: Powder-puff tutu

Costume designer of the New York City Ballet, Barbara Karinska (see page 15), in collaboration with the choreographer George Balanchine, created the powder-puff tutu in the late 1940s. Balanchine wanted a tutu that revealed more of the dancer's movements, so these tutus used shorter lengths of tulle with no hoop, creating a shorter, lighter effect.

4: Pointe shoe

The modern pointe shoe enables the dancer to stay on the tips of their toes for extended periods.

a) **Toe box** To give the toes the support they need to stand *en pointe*, sheets of leather were originally used to build the toe box, but it is now created from layer upon layer of paper and fabric glued together.

b) **Platform** The end of the shoe that contains the toe box.

c) **Ribbons** Pointe shoes are covered in pale satin, and ribbons of the same fabric are sewn on to keep the shoe in place. A dancer must learn the correct way to tie the ribbons.

d) **Outer sole** This is made of leather either scraped or buffed to ensure traction on the dance floor.

e) **Insole**, also known as the shank.

f) **Vamp** Covering the top of the foot and the metatarsals, dancers can request a high or low vamp depending on their instep. The vamp can be adjusted to ensure the correct tightness.

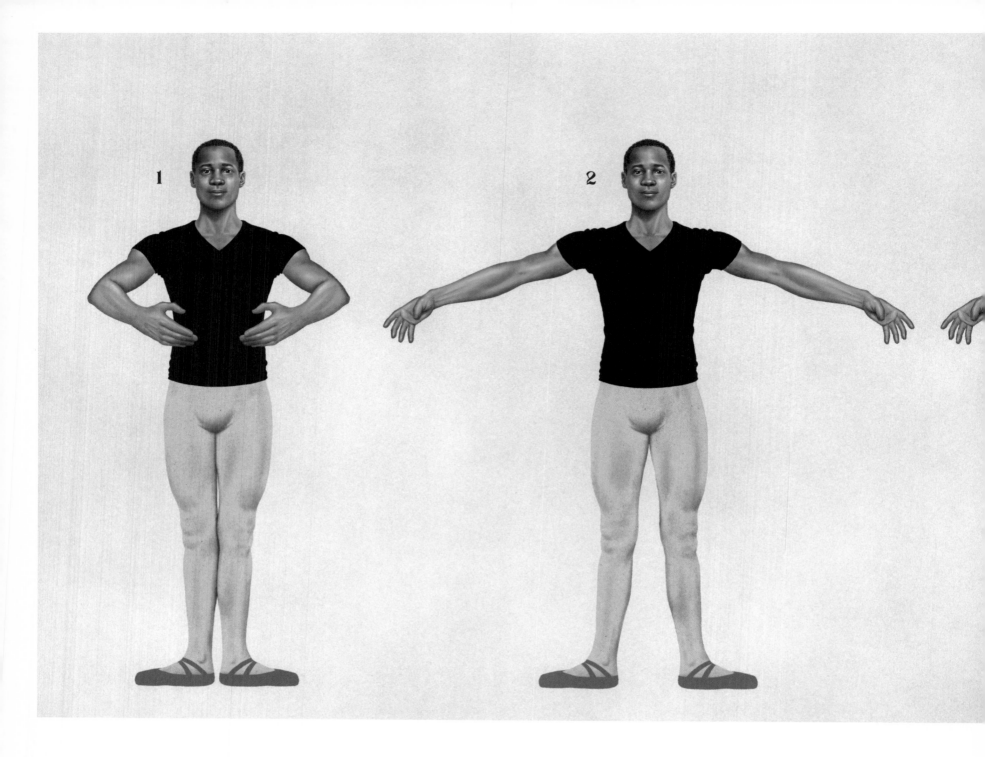

Ballet Positions

Ballet is considered the most graceful of all dance forms. From perfectly composed posture to seamless movement, ballet has survived for many centuries as a dance technique because it has solid foundations that dancers use to build on strength, technique and poise.

The five positions of ballet form the fundamentals of classical ballet technique. They are widely believed to have been invented by the French dancer and choreographer Pierre Beauchamp (1631–1705), ballet tutor to King Louis XIV (see page 19). Beginning with the positions of the feet, which are matched by the arms, these positions are known as first through fifth. In all positions, body weight is evenly distributed over both feet, which can either remain flat on the floor, rest on the balls of the feet (demi pointe), or rest on the toes (pointe). Professional ballet dancers are required to practise them every day to ensure they have the discipline required to carry out every other movement.

There are some other basic moves and techniques that need to be mastered. Those seen most often in performances are the *jeté*, or jump, *arabesque* (where a dancer stands on one

leg with the other extended straight behind the body), *pirouette* (where the dancer turns many times on one leg, *en pointe*), and *bourrée* (rapid movement of the feet when *en pointe*).

These basic movements form the words of ballet, and choreographers use these words in different ways to create the sentences and paragraphs that become the movement phrases of a ballet production.

Now Showing

1: First position
The heels are together with toes turned outwards until the feet are in a straight line. The arms are held in front of the body in a slightly raised position. The elbows are rounded.

2: Second position
The feet are in a parallel line at a distance of approximately 30cm. The arms are held out horizontally, with shoulders, wrists and hands bending downwards.

3: Third position
The heel of one foot rests against the instep of the other; both are firmly turned out. One arm is kept in first position in front of the body, while the other is held to the side in second position.

4: Fourth position
One foot rests about 30cm in front of the other; both are turned out. The feet are shown crossed here, but can also be open. One arm is kept in second position, while the other is raised above the head.

5: Fifth position
The feet are turned out and pressed closely together; the heel of one foot against the toes of the other. Both arms are raised above the head.

The Three Great Ballets

The late 19th century was a golden era for the Russian ballet under the Imperial reign of Alexander III (1845–1894). Marius Petipa (1818–1910) was director and chief choreographer of the Imperial Russian ballet from 1871, and Petipa and his assistant, Lev Ivanov (1834–1901), collaborated with the composer Pyotr Ilyich Tchaikovsky (1840–1893) to create three 'story' ballets (ballets that have a plot and characters). Extraordinarily, they were all created and premiered within five years of each other, and are still the most performed ballets today.

The first, *The Sleeping Beauty*, premiered in 1890 in Saint Petersburg and was a lavish production with sets and scenery showing off the luxury of Imperial Russia. Tchaikovsky's ballet was based on Charles Perrault's fairy tale *La Belle au bois dormant*, which also inspired the famous tale by the Brothers Grimm. The ballet focuses on two conflicting forces – the good Lilac Fairy and the evil Carabosse. Although initially favourably received (the Tsar apparently described it as 'very nice'), Tchaikovsky unfortunately died three years later, and so didn't live to see the great success it eventually became.

The Sleeping Beauty was followed in quick succession by *The Nutcracker* in 1892. When Petipa fell ill during the creation, choreography assistant Ivanov stepped in to help. Set in the cosiness of Christmas, inside the beautifully decorated Saint Petersburg drawing rooms, it is no surprise that this ballet has become the seasonal offering for every production company in the world.

Swan Lake premiered in 1895 (see pages 28–29) and was the last in this trio of choreographic and musical masterpieces. These, and other full-length ballets such as *Giselle*, *Don Quixote* and *Coppelia*, form the core of the classical ballet repertoire. They are the stories that audiences want to watch over and over again and provide the platform for the greatest ballet dancers in the world to show off their skills.

Now Showing

The Nutcracker premiered 18 December 1892 at the Imperial Mariinsky Theatre in Saint Petersburg
Original choreography by Marius Petipa and Lev Ivanov | Original music by Pyotr Ilyich Tchaikovsky
Shown in artwork: Sir Peter Wright production, Royal Ballet, London, 1991

A former principal ballerina with The Royal Ballet, Darcey Bussell (born 1969) became one of the audience's favourite dancers at the Royal Ballet and a role model for many young aspiring dancers. She featured for many years in *The Nutcracker* and other classical roles. Here, she is performing as the Sugar Plum Fairy.

Rudolf Nureyev

"Lights go out and I die,
tomorrow I will be born again,
tomorrow I will dance again."

Considered by many as the greatest male ballet dancer of his generation, Rudolf Nureyev (1938–1993) set the ballet world alight with his exuberance and grace: his athletic leaps and spins almost convinced the audience he was flying!

Born on a train on the Trans-Siberian railway, Nureyev endured much hardship and poverty during his childhood, and was evacuated from Moscow to Ufa during the Second World War. His lifelong love affair with ballet began at age six, when his mother took him to see a performance called The Crane Song at their local theatre.

Nureyev joined the world-famous Kirov Ballet (now called the Mariinsky Ballet) in 1958. His talent and passion impressed quickly but he also gained a reputation for being disruptive. When the company went on tour to Paris in 1961 at the height of the Cold War, Nureyev refused to obey the rules set by the political agents running the show. The tour was due to continue to London but, upon arrival at the airport, Nureyev was ordered to return to Moscow. He dramatically leaped into the arms of French police, declaring 'I want to be free!' Just a week later, he performed in The Sleeping Beauty at the Théâtre des Champs-Élysées and received a standing ovation. His defection was big news around the world however, and meant Nureyev completely left his life in Russia behind.

By 1963, Nureyev had become an international star. He captivated audiences with his charismatic performances and quickly revived the role of the male ballet dancer. For so long the ballerina had been at the centre of all the great ballets, but Nureyev's combination of strength and elegance changed the focus.

Despite being a confident soloist, Nureyev had many dancing partners, most famously Margot Fonteyn (1919–1991). Nineteen years older than Nureyev, Fonteyn was considering retirement in 1961 but was intrigued by Nureyev and so agreed to dance with him. Their extraordinary onstage chemistry resulted in the perfect partnership. In Kenneth MacMillan's rendition of Romeo and Juliet, which premiered in 1965, the duo were applauded by the audience for a staggering 40 minutes.

▷ ——— NOW SHOWING ——— ◁

Rudolf Nureyev as Prince Florimund in The Sleeping Beauty | Royal Opera House, London, 1966

The third act in The Sleeping Beauty is the chance for any male ballet dancer to show off their virtuosity, as it ends in great leaps around the stage and breathtaking turns. Nureyev took every opportunity to show his skills at these moments, much to the delight of the audience.

Swan Lake

Swan Lake is one of the most performed ballets in the world, famously choreographed to the music of Pyotr Ilyich Tchaikovsky by Marius Petipa (see page 24) and Russian ballet dancer Lev Ivanov in 1895. It tells the tale of Prince Siegfried who falls in love with a young woman, Odette, who has been turned into a swan by the evil Baron von Rothbart. At a palace ball, Siegfried is tricked into thinking that Odile (the daughter of Rothbart) is his betrothed and asks for her hand in marriage. Realising his terrible mistake, Siegfried and Odette end their lives in the shimmering waters of Swan Lake.

One of the most famous 'white ballets', which include scenes where the mostly female *corps de ballet* are dressed in white and perform in unison, *Swan Lake* has many characteristics of productions from the 19th century – the fight between good and evil, the parallel existence of the real and spirit (or animal) world, and the use of disguise leading to mistaken identity.

There are two main reasons why this ballet has remained so popular – the first is the romantic score of Tchaikovsky, which swells our hearts as the tragic tale is told and reaches its climax. The second is the extraordinary imagery of the white swans hovering in precise unison – a chance to show off the extraordinary skills of the *corps de ballet* in any company. For many people, *Swan Lake is* ballet!

While choreographers stayed faithful to the classic *Swan Lake* for many years, there have been a number of more recent reinterpretations. Fredrik Rydman's *Swan Lake: Reloaded* saw street dance choreography combined with Tchaikovsky's score, while Alexander Ekman's version recreated a real lake on the stage! Perhaps the most famous recent interpretation of *Swan Lake*, however, is that by Sir Matthew Bourne (see pages 48–49). Instead of featuring graceful, gentle swans, Bourne's are performed by male dancers and are much more aggressive, as real swans often are.

Now Showing

Swan Lake premiered 4 March 1877 at the Bolshoi Theatre, Moscow
Original choreography by Julius Reisinger | Original music by Pyotr Ilyich Tchaikovsky
Shown in artwork: Kansas City Ballet production, Missouri, 2016

The Dance of the Cygnets is always one of the audience's favourite moments in *Swan Lake*. In this late addition to the choreography, the dancers imitate the way that young swans huddle together for protection and dance in unison. The coordination required must be exact while maintaining elegant poise, and so it is one of the most challenging sections of the ballet.

Carlos Acosta

"Don't remain where you are, but keep evolving."

Carlos Acosta (born 1973) is the living incarnation of the phrase 'dream big'. One of the world's best ballet dancers, he has appeared in almost every classical male role from Spartacus to Romeo, with a career in classical ballet spanning 28 years. The story of Acosta's rise to fame is nothing short of a modern-day fairy tale.

Born in Cuba, Acosta was the youngest of eleven children growing up in one of Havana's most deprived districts. Acosta's father, a truck driver, encouraged his son to audition for the National Ballet School of Havana, knowing it might change the family's fortunes. It was to become the first step in a hugely successful international ballet career. Undoubtedly influenced by Cuba's rich and vibrant dance scene, Acosta, already a talented break-dancer, went on to win a clutch of awards and dance at some of the world's most prestigious companies, including the Houston Ballet in Texas and the Royal Ballet in London.

Known for his exceptional athleticism and dynamic stage presence, Acosta's performances lit up any room. Highly innovative and acrobatic, Acosta became the English National Ballet's youngest ever principal dancer, aged just 18, and in 2003 became the Royal Ballet's first Black principal.

After dancing his last classical ballet performance in 2015, Acosta sought opportunities outside of the Royal Ballet. A talented director and choreographer, he had already created several award-winning ballets, including the semi-autobiographical *Tocororo* (2003), but in 2015 he created his own company, Acosta Danza, offering opportunities for other dancers and choreographers from Cuba. In 2020, he took over as the artistic director of Birmingham Royal Ballet.

▷ ── Now Showing ──◁

Carlos Acosta performs in *Requiem* | Royal Opera House, London, 2006

Ballet dancer, choreographer and Royal Ballet artistic director Sir Kenneth MacMillan (1929–1992) created *Requiem* for the German Stuttgart Ballet in 1976 as a tribute to his friend John Cranko who had been the director at Stuttgart and had died two years earlier. McMillan used Gabriel Fauré's *Requiem* as the score and the dancers portray mourners, angels and spirits. Both McMillan and costume designer Yolanda Sonnabend (1935–2015) were influenced by the drawings and paintings of William Blake, although here Acosta wears a loin cloth depicting a biblical figure.

The Ballets Russes

After the glorious years of the early 19th century, the next major moment in the development of dance and ballet came with the founding of the ballet company the Ballets Russes in 1909 by the great art critic Serge Diaghilev (1872–1929). After a career in visual art and publishing, Diaghilev left his native Saint Petersburg to settle in Paris and brought together some of the most gifted choreographers, designers and composers of the time. The Ballet Russes proved to be a dramatically different approach to dance-making.

Diaghilev was a master at bringing together creatives, including the composers Igor Stravinsky (1882–1971), Claude Debussy (1862–1918) and Richard Strauss (1864–1949), while Pablo Picasso and Coco Chanel were among the artists and designers to comment and advise during the company's fashion parades. The company became equally famous for its set and costume designs as for its music and choreography, and the collaborations led to some of the masterpieces of the 20th century, including *Le Sacre du Printemps* (*The Rite of Spring*).

The public, however, were not quite ready for the radical nature of some of these new works and there was famously a near riot at the premiere of the *The Rite of Spring* in Paris on the 29 May 1913. Aside from the ballet depicting a ceremony where a young girl is sacrificed to ensure the success of the year's harvest, Stravinsky's avant-garde score was a complete departure from musical tradition, and Vaslav Nijinsky's (1889–1950) choreography featured strange stamping movements and awkward poses. According to reports at the time, the dancers could hardly hear the orchestra against the shouts of disapproval from the audience.

Despite initial controversy, the Ballets Russes toured all over the world and many of the dancers and choreographers went on to make their own mark on ballet history, including the great George Balanchine (see page 35). The company disbanded after Diaghilev's death in 1929, but reformed in Monte Carlo in 1931.

Now Showing

The Rite of Spring premiered 29 May 1913 at the Théâtre des Champs-Élysées
Choreography by Vaslav Nijinsky | Music by Igor Stravinsky
Shown in artwork: The Joffrey Ballet production, Los Angeles, 1987

There have been over 200 different productions of *The Rite of Spring* but the original choreography was only danced eight times during its original run and, because Diaghilev and Nijinsky fell out, the ballet was rechoreographed. The Joffrey Ballet set about the painstaking task of reconstructing the ballet, and while it took 16 years to piece together the lost choreography, it was eventually performed in 1987.

Abstract Ballet

In the 20th century, a new form of ballet emerged that was to challenge all that had gone before. Abstract ballet explored patterns and formations in choreography, with an emphasis on movement and visual impact instead of narrative. Although many story ballets are still performed and remain popular, most new contemporary ballets are abstract and are performed typically in a 'triple bill', which means three short works are performed in the same evening.

Arguably the first famous abstract ballet is *Les Sylphides* (1909), created by Russian choreographer Michel Fokine (1880–1942). It was commissioned for the Ballet Russes (see page 32) and first danced by a star-studded cast that included Anna Pavlova and Vaslav Nijinsky. In the performance, set to the emotive music of Frédéric Chopin (1810–1849), a young man is out walking at night when he comes across a group of white sylphs (female spirits of the air). The man – sometimes portrayed as a poet dreaming about his inspirations – dances with

the sylphs creating a dreamy, romantic mood. The characters take a back seat to the music, with each of the female dancers being named after their style of movement.

Despite Fokine's success, the king of the abstract ballet was about to be crowned. Previously part of the Ballet Russes, in 1948 choreographer George Balanchine co-founded the New York Ballet. Determined to only make abstract ballets, Balanchine wanted 'dance to be the star of the show'. He introduced movements and qualities from other genres, including musicals, resulting in dancers who moved with more attitude, often dancing just off the beat rather than on it. His particular style of choreography became known as the Balanchine technique; it demanded immaculate musical timing, intense speed and longer lines.

Now Showing

Jewels premiered 13 April 1967 at The New York State Theatre in New York | Choreography by George Balanchine | Music by Gabriel Fauré (Emeralds), Igor Stravinsky (Rubies) and Pyotr Ilyich Tchaikovsky (Diamonds) | Shown in artwork: The New York City Ballet production, New York City, 2018

Balanchine's first full length abstract ballet was *Jewels*. At the suggestion of Arnold Van Cleef, owner of the jewellers Van Cleef & Arpels, he created three acts inspired by a different precious stone. With music by a different composer, each act evokes a distinct mood. Emeralds, shown here, conveys the elegance of France. *Jewels* remains one of the masterpieces of the abstract ballet repertoire.

STAGE 2

CONTEMPORARY

Contemporary Dance • Martha Graham • Trisha Brown
Akram Khan • Pina Bausch • Sir Matthew Bourne

STAGE 2

CONTEMPORARY

Contemporary Dance • Martha Graham • Trisha Brown
Akram Khan • Pina Bausch • Sir Matthew Bourne

Contemporary Dance

At the beginning of the 20th century, an art revolution called Modernism was sweeping across Western Europe and the United States. After the shock of the First World War (1914–1918), artists from all disciplines wanted to move forward and kick against some of the traditions of the past.

Dance was caught up in this revolution and, in the 1920s and 30s, a genre called modern dance appeared, pioneered mostly by female choreographers in Europe and the United States, including Ruth St. Denis (1879–1968), Isadora Duncan (1877–1927), Mary Wigman (1886–1973) and, perhaps the most important contemporary choreographer of all, Martha Graham (see pages 40–41). These revolutionaries wanted to replace constrictive dance techniques, such as ballet, with freer movements that were more akin to the body's natural state. They were eager to demonstrate the capabilities of women in dance and actively worked against outdated notions – delicate, mute, laced and corseted – to portray liberated, spirited, thought-provoking performers.

These women were at the forefront of a new way of thinking, which is now known as contemporary dance. It is a wide term that encompasses many different styles and approaches, from the more restrained style of American choreographer Merce Cunningham (1919–2009), through to the dramatic *Tantztheater* (dance theatre) of German Pina Bausch (see pages 46–47), and everything in between.

Today, there are many outstanding dancers and choreographers working in this field, each with a unique identity. The basic rule in contemporary dance is that there are no rules, except the ones the choreographer makes up. Once the curtains rise, anything can happen during a contemporary dance – and it often does!

NOW SHOWING

A dancer performs in *Beach Birds,* premiered 20 June 1991 at Theatre 11, Zurich | Choreographed by Merce Cunningham | Costume, set and lighting design by Marsha Skinner | Music by John Cage

Merce Cunningham regularly collaborated with the composer John Cage. They developed a unique way of working where the music and choreography were created completely separately and only came together in the first performance. This meant the dancers were no longer tied to the rhythms of the music; the two art forms stood alone but shared a common space.

Beach Birds was more fluid than other Cunningham dances and meant each performance ended up being a different length. He said of the choreography, "The dancers don't have to be exactly together. They can dance like a flock of birds, when they suddenly take off." Cunningham was always fascinated by the movement of birds and in his last years spent most of his time sketching them.

"Dancers are
the messengers
of the gods."

Martha Graham

Born in 1894 in Pennsylvania, Martha Graham showed an early interest in dance, but her parents did not approve of her becoming a dancer. It was only after her father's death in 1914 that Graham, then aged 20, was able to pursue her dream and enrolled at the Denishawn school in Los Angeles. The eventual pioneer and creator of modern dance, Graham allowed and encouraged women to be at the forefront of artistic achievement.

Graham created a dance technique that allowed the performers to become aware of, and use, their gravity, as opposed to ballet where the emphasis was on the dancers appearing weightless. Graham also worked on the principle of 'contracting and release'. In her choreography, movement comes from the tension of pulling in, or 'contracting', the pelvic muscles and curving the spine. The flow of energy is then 'released' from the body when it straightens. When repeated, this gives a rhythmic flow to the movement, a cycle similar to breathing in and out, but with more exaggerated movements. It was used in many of Graham's greatest choreographies, including the solo dance *Lamentation* and larger group works such as *Chronicle* (1936). It is still practised as a daily class in many dance companies and schools today.

The main themes of Graham's work include Greek mythology and American history. While her early works featured only female dancers, men joined Graham's company in 1938, prompting her to explore new themes. For example, the staged work *Appalachian Spring* (1944) explores the experiences of early American pioneers, but also the act of falling in love.

By presenting ideas and images that were unfamiliar, Graham introduced a new era in dance. She collaborated with composers such as Louis Horst and the fashion designers Calvin Klein and Donna Karan. She taught actors including Liza Minnelli and Gregory Peck and inspired future dance greats such as Merce Cunningham (see page 39) and Twyla Tharp.

▷ ──── Now Showing ──── ◁

Martha Graham stars in *Lamentation*, premiered 8 January 1930 at Maxine Elliot's Theatre, New York City | Choreographed by Martha Graham | Music by Zoltán Kodály

Lamentation, sometimes referred to as the Dance of Sorrow, is a four-minute solo piece first performed by Graham herself. The costume was deliberately designed to restrict her movements and to enhance the expression of grief, but also to highlight its boundaries.

Trisha Brown

In the mid 1960s, something extraordinary was happening in downtown Manhattan. A group of dancers, visual artists and musicians had taken over the Judson Memorial Church in Greenwich Village as a creative experiment. One of the leading lights in this new movement was the American choreographer and dancer Trisha Brown. Born in 1936, Brown studied modern dance at the Mills College in California and also studied in the studio of modern dance pioneer Merce Cunningham (see page 39).

Brown and the other Judson artists rejected the restraints of modern dance practice and choreography basics, instead opting for something much more unpredictable. In doing so, they created the foundations of postmodern dance, one of the most exciting new genres to emerge in a generation. Brown became inspired by the everyday, often working with completely untrained dancers and members of the public to create her pieces.

In 1970, Brown founded the Trisha Brown Dance company and started to experiment with dance in very unusual settings: around the rooftops of buildings or even climbing up the sides of buildings (using ropes and harnesses!). She wanted to take dance out into the public

realm so that all could participate. Around this time, Brown also created seminal works such as *Accumulation* (1971). This piece tested the dancers' memory and concentration, starting with one gesture and adding another and then another throughout the five-minute piece.

During the 1980s, Brown began working on large-scale stage productions, including *Set and Reset*. Often cited as one of the central pieces in the postmodern dance cannon, it brought Brown international fame. She received nearly every award available to contemporary choreographers, and today the Trisha Brown Dance Company continues to perform her work.

▷ ——————————— **Now Showing** ——————————— ◁

Set and Reset premiered 20 October 1983 at Brooklyn Academy of Music, New York
Original choreography by Trisha Brown | Original costume and set design by Robert Rauschenberg
Original music by Laurie Anderson | Shown in artwork: Dancers perform in *Set and Reset/Reset*,
Candoco Dance Company production, 2021

Set and Reset is a modern masterpiece. Featuring the designs of American artist Robert Rauschenberg (1925–2008) and a hypnotic score by musician and performer Laurie Anderson (born 1947), the piece was created by Brown by asking the dancers to improvise, or make up, patterns of movement. She would observe and choose those that were most interesting to her and then create a set work that would be performed the same way each night. And so, although the performance may look like the dancers are improvising, the movement patterns are in fact completely fixed. The choreography has a wonderful looseness and flow that could only be the result of making a dance this way. Candoco, a UK-based production company that celebrates disability in dance, began recreating and adapting this work in 2011.

Akram Khan

With a compelling and powerful stage presence and a distinctive fast-paced and technically complex dance style, Anglo-Bengali choreographer Akram Khan (born 1974) is one of the most important contemporary dancers working today and is known for pushing artistic boundaries and wowing audiences.

Born in south London to Bangladeshi parents, Khan showed early promise as a dancer. He quickly learned to blend his heritage with the pop culture of vibrant London, fusing his Kathak technique (a traditional form of South Asian dance – see page 69) with influences from Michael Jackson's MTV videos and Bruce Lee's karate moves.

At just 13 years old, Khan was recruited to perform in Peter Brook's *Mahabharata,* a legendary nine-hour play based on the Indian epic. This experience heavily influenced Khan, introducing him to the craft of art direction, but also emphasising the importance of rooting his performances in tradition and the storytelling of his heritage.

After studying contemporary dance, Khan soon found success in both the London and international dance scene. Performing his first solo works in the late 1990s, he displayed incredible power in the fast-turning spins so inherent in the Kathak style. These turns combined with intense rhythmic footwork to give Khan a truly unique dance language.

Also known for his storytelling, Khan's most career-defining moment can perhaps be seen in his choreography for the opening of the 2012 London Olympics. Watched by a global audience of 900 million viewers, Khan created a moving tribute to the victims of the July 2005 London bombings with over 100 dancers. The performance poignantly ended with Khan duetting with a young boy of South Asian heritage, as if a mirror to his younger self.

Often involved in high-profile and fascinating collaborations with actors, musicians, artists and writers, Khan continues to astound audiences around the world.

NOW SHOWING

Akram Khan performs in *Zero Degrees*, premiered 8 July 2005 at Sadler's Wells Theatre, London
Choreography by Sidi Larbi Cherkaoui and Akram Khan | Set design by Sir Antony Gormley
Music by Nitin Sawhney

A deeply personal and moving performance that asks questions about identity and belonging, *Zero Degrees* is a collaboration between Khan and Cherkaoui. Inspired by their own dual identities (both are from Islamic families and grew up in Europe), *Zero Degrees* tells the story of a harrowing train journey Khan took from Bangladesh to India where he was hassled by border officials. British sculptor Sir Antony Gormley created life-sized copies of the two dancers that turned a duet into a piece for four characters. Set in a plain white cube, the dummies act as alter-egos to Khan and Cherkaoui.

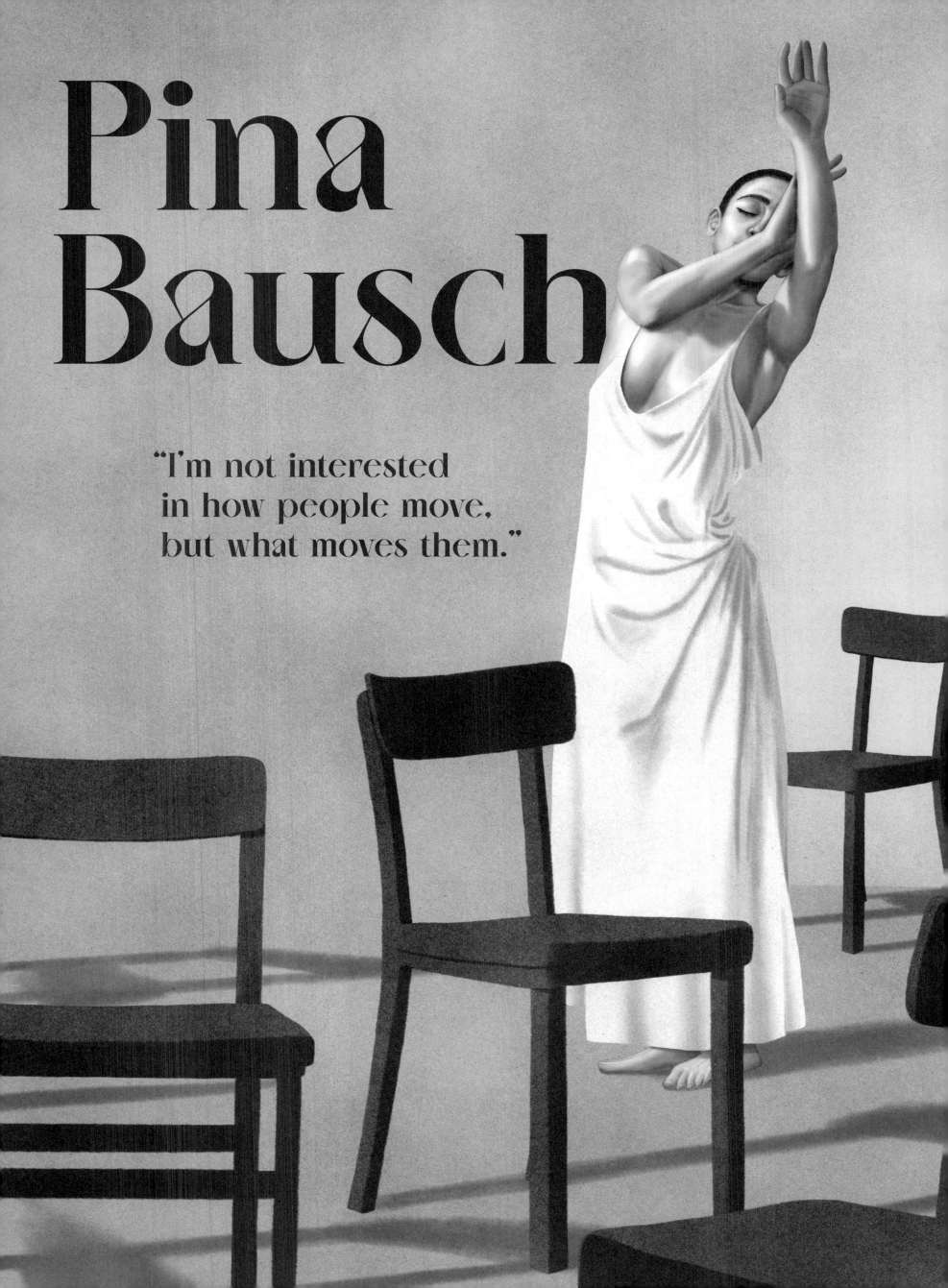

Pina Bausch

"I'm not interested
in how people move,
but what moves them."

Through the history of the arts, there are some who create more than great work – they revolutionise their art form in some way and influence a whole generation. In dance, one of those great artists was Pina Bausch.

Born in Germany in 1940, Bausch started her dance career at the Folkwangschule (now Folkwang University of the Arts) in Essen. From there, she won a three-year scholarship to New York's Juilliard school. Performing with both modern dance groups and the Metropolitan Ballet, Bausch developed her own distinct way of moving, particularly the elegant articulation of the arms sweeping high above her head.

In 1973, Bausch was asked to run the ballet company based in the Wuppertal Opera House, a little-known theatre in the German Ruhr Valley, alongside her collaborator Rolf Börzik (1944–1980). Amid an atmosphere of experimentation and revolution, the duo began creating radical works.

Known as *Tanztheater,* or dance theatre, these dances were unlike anything seen before. Dancers were encouraged to express their emotions through theatre techniques and movement. Bausch encouraged her performers to speak during performances, and often depicted cruelty and struggle. Early Wuppertal audiences were often shocked and disgusted by this new unconventional style, but Bausch remained undeterred and continued to be provocative throughout her career. Her creation of *Tanztheater* allowed the choreography that followed to be much freer and experimental.

The surrealism in Bausch's works famously extended to costume and set design, and she included a literal depiction of a crumbling brick wall in *Palermo Palermo* (1989). Her tenacity, talent and vision made Bausch one of the most significant choreographers in modern dance. She left a legacy of over 50 productions which will stand the test of time.

Now Showing

Pina Bausch stars in *Café Müller*, premiered 20 May 1978 at Wuppertal Opera House, Wuppertal
Choreography by Pina Bausch | Set design by Rolf Börzik | Music by Henry Purcell

Picture a young girl hiding under the tables of her parents' café well past her bedtime, observing the comings and goings of the adults around her. That young girl was Philippine, or 'Pina' Bausch. Her early observations in her parents' café would play a significant part in her work, with its mastery of human interactions. *Café Müller* is the clearest representation of those childhood memories, with performers eerily moving through the darkness, pushing café chairs away as if ghosts in a dream.

Sir Matthew Bourne

For many years, the stories of the classics of the ballet repertoire remained generally untouched. That is until the arrival of choreographer Sir Matthew Bourne (born 1960), who revisited and radically reimagined them.

Bourne was raised in London by a working-class family. His mother had a love of theatre and encouraged Bourne to travel by bus to the West End from a young age. He continued his interest in theatre into adulthood, working at one point in the bookshop in the National Theatre. Aged 22, Bourne began his studies at the Trinity Laban Conservatoire of Music and Dance. He started his first dance company, Adventures in Motion Pictures, in 1987.

Bourne's first large-scale commission was for *Nutcracker!* His version opened not in the opulent parlour of an upper-class household, but in an orphanage from which the protagonist is rescued. Similarly, his adaptation of *Sleeping Beauty* is first set in the Edwardian era, but after her 100-year sleep, the Beauty wakes up in the present day, the narrative enhanced by the introduction of vampires to the plot! But it was Bourne's brilliant idea to turn the usual ethereal female swans in *Swan Lake* into powerful – and at times viscous – male versions of the creatures that proved to be his breakthrough success. The image of the muscular torsos with white feathered leggings soon became iconic images. The Prince in Bourne's *Swan Lake* also falls in love with the male lead swan, which was controversial at the time of opening in 1995.

Blending different dance genres, including ballet, contemporary and musical theatre, and always adding his signature wit, Bourne is known as the most inventive choreographer of his generation. He has also become the most successful, with *Swan Lake* the longest-running ballet in both London's West End and on Broadway.

Now Showing

Ashley Shaw and Dominic North from the New Adventures Company perform in *Edward Scissorhands*, premiered 14 November 2005 at Theatre Royal, Plymouth, UK | Direction and choreography by Sir Matthew Bourne Set and costume design by Lez Brotherston | Music by Danny Elfman and Terry Davies

Adapted from Tim Burton's film of the same name, Bourne's theatrical interpretation of *Edward Scissorhands* is set in 1950s America. Prim, pretty and proper, the picturesque town and its perfect inhabitants contrast with the gothic, and at times disturbing, Edward Scissorhands – the creation of a scientist who tragically dies before his work has been completed. The wordless performance captures the isolation of Edward as he struggles to find his place in a town that doesn't understand him.

Perhaps the most moving scene is the beautiful duet between Edward and his sweetheart, Kim. As the couple fall in love, the viewer feels both elation and deep sadness for Edward, as he tenderly dances with Kim while avoiding touching her with his razor-sharp blades.

FOLK

Folk Dance • Flamenco • Antonio Gades
Irish Dancing • Morris Dancing

Folk Dance

At the heart of the folk tradition is the passing on of songs, music and dances that have never been formally written down. Instead, they pass from one generation to the next, often in informal settings. There are no codes or rules to be followed; they evolve as they are handed down. A folk dance can be seen as a long-established expression of the traditions and way of life of a particular country or region.

These traditional dances often have a social purpose and are part of a celebration or gathering – a wedding, a feast day or celebrating the harvest. The folk dance Bhangra, for example, began in the farming regions of Punjab in South Asia to celebrate the spring harvest festival Baisakhi. Hemp, or *bhang*, was often harvested, giving the dance its name.

An art form of the people – not controlled or ordained by the powers of government or the religious hierarchy – folk dances have historically been important in bringing people together, especially during times of hardship or upheaval. Irish step dancing (see pages 58–59) is the perfect example of how a folk dance not only reinforced a national identity but also had elements of rebellion within it, during a time of unrest. Flamenco (see pages 54–55) meanwhile originated from the struggles of the poorer parts of society in southern Spain.

Sometimes a folk dance becomes so intrinsically linked to its country's history it becomes the official national dance, for example Turkey's Halay which is performed at weddings, and England's Morris dancing (see pages 60–61). While Morris dancing has very much maintained its amateur status, others, such as Irish and Flamenco dance, have been taken to formal settings of the stage and theatre, becoming much more popular and sophisticated than their humble beginnings.

Now Showing

A male bhangra dancer performs with a khunda during a festival | Mississauga, Canada 2018

Energetic, lively and colourful, bhangra is the embodiment of the joy felt at harvest time. Full of leaps, kicks, and expressive arm movements, bhangra is normally performed in groups to the accompanying beat of a dhol (a double-headed drum). It was traditionally performed by Sikh and Muslim farmers from the region, but today anyone can partake in bhangra performances.

Flamenco

Passionate and fiery, flamenco can be considered more than a dance style – it is a philosophy of life, a way of being that is expressed through the medium of dance and music. Flamenco singers and guitarists work in unison with the dancers to create a total experience.

While the origins of flamenco remain unclear, it is thought it came to the Andalusia region of Spain during the Roma migration from India between the 9th and 14th centuries. Flamenco evolved gradually, combining many different cultures and influences. Its songs often tell of the struggles of many of the poorer parts of society. To fully express the travails of life and love, the dance is appropriately passionate and dramatic.

Flamenco is known for its distinctive costumes – long trailing dresses and shawls alongside slim, sleek trousers and waistcoats. The way the dancers carry themselves is also unique. Men show off their masculinity, with the arrogance of bullfighters. Women move proudly, with expressive use of the arms. The rhythmic stamping of the feet, amplified by the hard heels of the flamenco shoes, is also a very familiar feature of the dance.

The most important aspect of any flamenco performance is the atmosphere that is created, usually starting with a series of slow movements with little flourishes encouraged by cries of 'Ole!' from the audience, which builds to a series of climaxes. This heightened sense of emotion or expression is called *duende*, and while hard to define, it is the total presence of the dancer on the stage and their ability to fully immerse themselves, and therefore the audience, in the performance. A similar state can be linked to some other dances (see page 75).

For a long time, flamenco was a family-focussed and outdoor event. In 1842, however, its golden era began when the legendary singer Silverio Franconetti (1831–1889) opened one of the first *café cantantes*. From the bars and cafés of Southern Spain, flamenco's popularity spread, and it can now be enjoyed in theatres all around the world.

Now Showing

1: Female flamenco dancer (*bailaora*)
Shown here wearing a traditional dress with a layered ruffled hem.

2: Hand fan (*pericón*)
When a flamenco dancer waves her fan vigorously, she is doing more than cooling herself down: she is signalling mock impatience or pride, usually ending with a dramatic snap. So famed are these fan movements, the English poet and playwright Joseph Addison once said, 'Men have swords, women have fans, and fans are probably an equally effective weapon.'

3: Shawl (*mantón de manila*)
The shawls used in flamenco become part of the choreography. They can be spun around the dancer in a whirl, flung in the air as an extension of the dancer's gestures, or dramatically wrapped around the body. These are often embellished with fringed edges and made from luxurious fabrics.

4: Castanets (*castañuelas*)
These musical instruments are made of two concave wooden shells tied together with string and hooked over the thumb. While one of the shells rests in the palm, the other is pressed against it by the fingers. The ensuing rapid percussive beat is used as a rhythmic accompaniment to the dance.

5: Shoes
The leather shoes worn in flamenco are a key tool in the armoury of the flamenco dancer. Both the strapped shoe worn by female performers and the boots worn by male dancers have nails embedded in the heel and toes, enhancing the percussive use of the shoe that forms such an instrumental part of the flamenco sound.

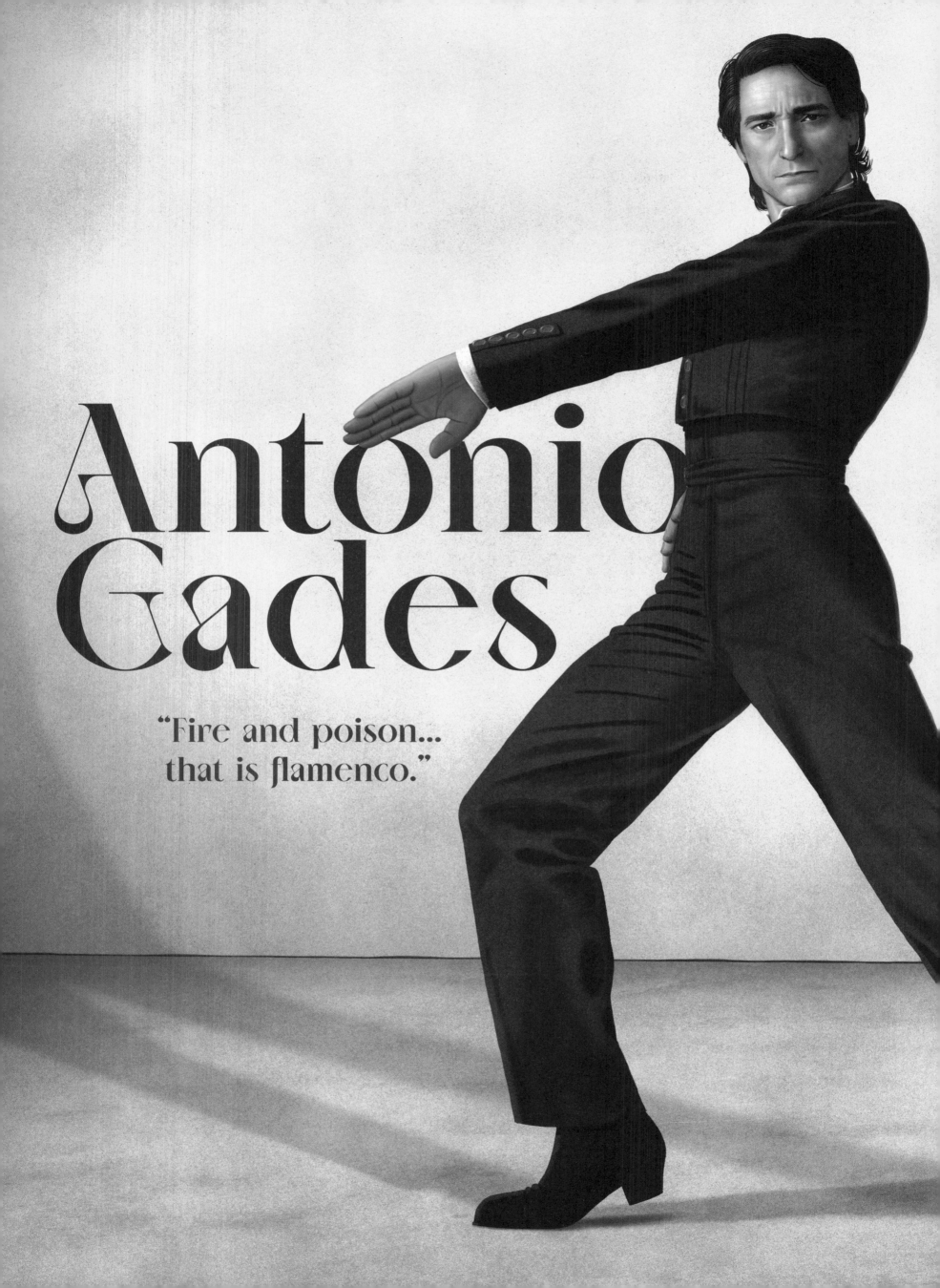

Antonio Gades

"Fire and poison...
that is flamenco."

There are few more famous flamenco dancers and choreographers than Antonio Gades (1936–2004). Known for his fierce passion, dedication and discipline, he is just as well known for his activism as he is for helping to popularise flamenco as an art form.

Born in Alicante, Spain, Gades grew up during one the most difficult periods in recent Spanish history. With the Spanish Civil War raging across the country, his father took up the call to arms and joined the fight, leaving the family desolate. Gades left school at just 11 years old to find work and help support his family, even finding a job as a bullfighter. He was already a promising dancer, however, and a local dance company in Madrid eventually recruited him, paving the way for the lengthy career he was about to embark upon.

Although he was to become a great flamenco dancer, Gades studied classical ballet and danced with many classical ballet companies, including Las Scala in Milan and the Royal Ballet in London. This education influenced his style: his faultless and elegant movements, posture and footwork commanded the stage.

But it is for his choreography that Gades will be most remembered. In 1981, Gades met the legendary film director Carlos Saura (1932–2023). Working together on three films, the duo brought flamenco to the big screen. *Bodas de Sangre* (1981) was a huge hit worldwide and was followed by *Carmen* (1983) and *El Amor Brujo* (1986). Gades' productions were epic, with large cast and sets and storytelling at their heart. Influenced by his socialist beliefs, his productions often told the struggles of the poor against the oppression of the state, particularly noticeable in his last work, *Fuenteovejuna* (1994).

Gades was a lifelong communist and spent most of his later years in Cuba. He died in 2004, aged 67. His legacy lives on through the Antonio Gades Foundation, which is based in Madrid.

▷ ─────── **Now Showing** ─────── ◁

Antonio Gades stars in *Bodas de Sangre (Blood Wedding)*,
released 9 March 1981, Spain | Directed by Carlos Saura

This film adaptation is based on Federico García Lorca's play of the same name. Gades and the others perform in a bare studio with minimum props. The tragedy of two men fighting for the love of one woman is told purely in the language of flamenco dance.

Irish Stepdance

There is perhaps no other dance that is more easily recognised as part of Irish culture than the stepdance. Identified by frantic footwork while the upper body remains rigid, accompanied by the lively sound of violins (informally known as 'fiddles') paired with beating drums, the spirited stepdance has transfixed audiences around the world.

Various theories abound about why Irish stepdance is characterised by its motionless arm movements. One suggestion is the influence of the Catholic church. The roots of Irish dancing stem from ancient rituals performed by the Celts and druids, but with the introduction of Christianity in the 5th century came different attitudes, and holding hands with a dance partner was frowned upon. Other theories suggest that movement became more restricted as dancers often performed on tables or barrel-tops. Most likely, however, is the influence of the dance masters, or travelling teachers, of the 18th century who preferred a restrained posture.

The competitive nature of stepdance also stems from this time. Each dance master had to stay within a specific district and so each region developed their own style of dance. When masters met at fairs, they would challenge each other to public dance contests. In 1893, the Gaelic league was founded to promote all aspects of Irish culture and began to organise formal competitions.

The characteristics of stepdance today make it a joy to watch. There are still traces of its druid origins, with dancers often performing in rings or lines as their ancestors once did, and carefully co-ordinated accentuated jumps, kicks, and quick and precise legwork.

Productions such as the phenomenally successful *Riverdance* have helped secure the popularity of Irish dance around the world, particularly in the US, where many stepdance competitions are held.

Now Showing

**Michael Flatley and a lineup of dancers perform in *Riverdance*, premiered 9 February 1995
at Point Theatre, Dublin | Choreography by Michael Flatley and Jean Butler | Set design
by Alan Farquharson | Costume design by Joan Bergin | Music by Bill Whelan**

The first ever showing of *Riverdance* saw Michael Flatley and the other dancers performing in the interval of the Eurovision Song Contest in Dublin in 1994. An estimated 300 million people were watching worldwide, marking the beginning of its international success.

Morris Dancing

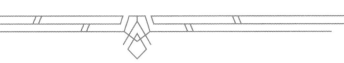

A uniquely English pastime, this lively and jovial folk dance is still performed in rural settings across England today, often as part of a festival or on special occasions, usually beginning on May Day (1 May) and continuing through the summer months. We do not know much about the timings of particular appearances before the 19th century, but a number were tied to Whitsun (the seventh Sunday after Easter), and others to particular local festivals or celebrations.

It is hard to pinpoint the true origins of Morris dancing, but it was recorded as far back as the 1400s and by the end of the 16th century it had become widely established as a form of entertainment. There are different styles of Morris dance associated with the specific area of England where they originated, including the Cotswolds region and the North West.

A Morris troupe is usually referred to as a side (or a team), but Morris dancing is nearly always an amateur affair and non-competitive. Morris dances are similar to many country dances, with performances made up of sequences of set patterns. These patterns normally involve dancers weaving in, out and around a partner. The difference with Morris dancing is that the dancers also wield wooden sticks. Integral to the dance is the clashing of these sticks while held high up in the air. A less aggressive form swaps sticks with handkerchiefs, which are waved and spun above the dancers' heads. The dancers also wear bells around their shins, and a variety of traditional instruments are used depending on the region.

The revival in Morris dancing around the beginning of the 20th century gave the impression for a number of years that the dance was a male-only tradition, but over the last 50 years this idea has mostly faded away and today it is thought that there are just as many female as male Morris dancers. There is even a female-only competitive form of the dance known as 'carnival' or 'fluffy' Morris.

Now Showing

Two Morris dancers perform at the Westminster Day of Dance | Trafalgar Square, London, 2018

It is impossible to miss a Morris dancing event as the costumes are always striking – ranging from fairly simple white shirts and trousers paired with coloured waistcoats and decorated hats, through to the more elaborate. The latter dress similarly to other ancient English folk traditions, including mummers (a troupe of amateur performers), and wear layers of torn material covering their whole bodies, often with painted faces.

DANCE–DRAMA

Dance–Drama • Khon
Indian Classical Dance • Kabuki

Dance–Drama

Throughout history, humans have always felt the need to tell stories – epic tales about nature or the origins of the world, of myths and legends, heroes and warriors, romance and tragedy, and the mysteries and magic of the gods. Many cultures across the world use dance to tell stories that are important to them. From the Hindu epic, the Ramayana, told through South Asian dance (see page 68) to the interplay of the real and spiritual world in Japanese kabuki (see pages 70–71), dance is perfectly placed to portray the spirituality, beauty and drama of these stories.

While many early dance-drama performances were religious in nature and performed in temples, they later moved to royal courts where the focus was on entertainment. Formed through ancient traditions, these stories are told in various ways: through movements that literally re-enact a particular series of events; the words of the music that accompany the dance; or a combination of the two. The purpose of dance-drama is not to purely narrate a series of events – this could easily be achieved through the words of a poem or play – but instead to use dance to bring the tales to life in ways which no other medium can, helping to evoke drama and emotion and connect with the audience.

The drama of these tales is also exaggerated using elaborate makeup or masks. In khon, for example, a traditional dance of Thailand (see pages 66–67), the dancers appear as mischievous monkeys or fearsome ogres with lifelike headdresses. Costumes can also be steeped in history, embellished and tweaked as the dance is handed down through the generations. Balinese legong, with its shimmering gold belts and collars and embellishments of gemstones and flowers, conveys the richness and splendour of the palaces and royal courts it was once associated with.

An essential part of their country's heritage, these beautiful dances are still studied and performed around the world, keeping the stories they tell very much alive.

Now Showing

Balinese dancer in traditional costume performing legong | Bali, Indonesia, 2005

Legong is an ancient court dance once performed in the royal palaces. According to legend, the dance materialised after a 19th century prince (the Prince of Sukawati) fell ill and had a dream in which two young nymphs danced to gamelan music. When he recovered his health, the prince ordered that the dance be performed according to his vision.

Khon

The traditional Thai dance khon is a true spectacle to behold. Combining dance, music, poetry and martial arts, khon dancers wear brightly coloured masks, elaborate costumes and headwear to tell the story of the Ramakien (the Thai version of the Ramayana), portraying fierce warriors and mythical creatures from this epic tale. While its history is hard to pinpoint, it is thought that khon dates back to the Ayutthaya period (1351–1767) and it is mentioned in Thai literature from 1529.

Khon is often described as 'masked pantomime' because the actors use gestures rather than lines to convey the plot, and are accompanied by narrators. The movement style is very ritualistic, with graceful hand gestures and a specific set of positions. The feet and knees are typically set wide apart in a stance common to martial arts disciplines. There are also athletic moments during the performance, with somersaults and human pyramids enhancing the most dramatic moments in the story. At other times, the dancers seem to glide around the stage, taking very small steps, leaving the impression that they are hovering like spirits.

Performances are often accompanied by a large piphat ensemble made up of a range of percussion and wind instruments. Khon, therefore, consists of a great many elements but each component – the dancers, the chorus, the soloists and the orchestra – are all co-ordinated and work seamlessly together.

Historically, khon was exclusively performed by men and only at the Thai royal court for members of the royal family. This royal connection is reflected in the lavish and painstaking costume designs. Today, however, it is learned and performed by many young people in Thailand. Threatened by the huge expense and amount of resources needed for just one performance, in 2018 khon was officially recognised by UNESCO who saw the need to protect this ancient art.

Now Showing

Dancers partake in a khon performance | Sala Chalermkrung Royal Theatre, Bangkok, 2019

The battle scenes in a khon performance diplay incredible combat choreography, drawing on traditions including martial arts, pole and sword fighting. An equally impressive part of the performance are the masks worn by the dancers. Khon mask making is a fine art, and makers need to be skilled in many areas in order to create just one mask. Skills involve paper working, wood carving, engraving, sculpting, leather working and goldsmithery. Just one mask made using these traditional methods can take three months.

Indian Classical Dance

India is a pioneer in the performing arts. With a rich cultural heritage, Indian classical dance, displaying drama, grace, spirituality and skill, is a proud reflection of the country's identity and today shares the international stage with some of the best dances in the world. There are generally considered to be ten Indian classical dances (Chhau, Bharatanatyam, Kathak, Kathakali, Kuchipudi, Manipuri, Mohiniyattam, Odissi, Sattriya and Yakshagana), and they all involve the telling of a story through dance and the use of gesture and expression.

Kathak, originating from the north of India, is an ancient form of dance dating back to 400 BCE. It began as a way of transmitting the stories and epic tales from Hinduism – particularly the story of Krishna, one of the most popular and revered gods – firstly from village to village, then to the temples and the Mughal court. This unique classical dance has strong influences from both Hindu and Islamic cultures. The pure dance aspect, known as nritta, is highly athletic. The dancer matches the rhythms of the musicians by stamping their feet and completing spectacularly fast spins of the body (similar to a pirouette in ballet) while simultaneously encircling the stage. Nritya (the expressive aspect of the dance) is conveyed through the eyes and facial expressions to increase the drama of the epic tales.

Bharatanatyam, originating from the south of India, was until the 19th century only performed in temples. This connection with the holy sites is no better illustrated than in the carvings that cover the walls of the 10th century Nataraja Temple in the south Indian state of Tamil Nadu. Here can be seen all the 108 postures which form the basis of this dance.

The nritta aspect in Bharatanatyam celebrates the beauty of strong lines in the body. In this dance, the legs are bent, and the arms and hands are elegantly positioned to bring about pleasing symmetry. The nritya is very detailed, recounting every twist and turn of the chosen Hindu text. Musical accompaniment is crucial to any Bharatanatyam performance, with a singer reciting verses and texts accompanied by the flute, violin and the double-sided drum, the mridangam.

Now Showing

A Kathak dancer performs at an event in Bharatiya Vidya Bhavan | Bangalore, 2018

The elegant, detailed and richly coloured Kathak costume is essential to the dance. Representing culture and tradition, they also exaggerate the storytelling and make sure that no detail goes unnoticed by the audience.

Percussion and music are also integral to Indian classical dance, and the sound of rhythmic bells, or ghungroos, not only create the atmosphere but add to the tempo. Tiny pea-shaped bells are attached to a leather strap and tied around the ankles of the dancer.

Kabuki

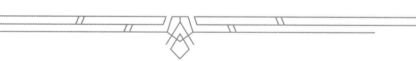

Kabuki is a classical form of dance-drama from Japan, celebrated for its dramatic makeup, beautiful costumes and exaggerated style of performance. The name 'kabuki' literally means 'song' (ka), 'dance' (bu) and 'skill' (ki), and the performance combines all three elements to tell stories through plays and abstract movement. Kabuki performers therefore must learn all three disciplines to graduate to the stage.

The first formally recognised show was performed in Kyoto around 1603. A priestess named Izumo no Okuni led a troupe of actresses around the region to raise money for a shrine. The actresses often played male roles and, although based on Buddhist prayer dances, the shows were romantic tales. Kabuki proved popular, but the government disliked the sensual nature of the dancing and, by 1629, women were banned from performing.

For a brief period, women were replaced by adolescent boys, but since 1652 adult men have exclusively performed kabuki, and continue to do so today. This includes onnagata — male performers who play female roles. Kabuki is a family business in Japan. The actors are the sons and grandsons of a whole generation of performers, who train from an early age and inherit

one of the family's performing names once they have reached the correct standard.

There are three main genres of kabuki. Pure dance performances are called *shosagoto,* and the emphasis is on storytelling and conveying meaning through movement and mime. *Jidaimono* are history plays and often portray legendary stories. *Sewamono* are modern tales that focus on the lives of ordinary people rather than mythical heroes. Kabuki, is actor-led rather than story-led and the aim is to ensure there is beauty in every aspect of the performance.

Kabuki remains Japan's most popular type of theatre. The onnagata actors of today are praised for their artistry and show off their grace and poise with slow delicate movements and hovering footwork. Kabuki stars still descend from established dynasties but today they often become huge celebrities in Japan and act in TV shows and films.

▷ ─────────────── **Now Showing** ─────────────── ◁

Fuji Musume (藤娘), The Wisteria Maiden, **premiered 1826 (ninth month), Nakamura-za, Edo, Japan**
Choreography by Fujima Taisuke | Music by Kineya Rokusaburô IV | Lyrics by Katsui Genpachi
Shown in artwork: Fujima Kanso II adaptation, Kabuki-za, Tokyo, 2006

Originally part of a five-part dance sequence, *Fuji Musume* is the only dance that has survived. The spirit of the wisteria tree
is shown in a painting, but upon seeing a young man pass by, she steps out of the painting and attempts to gain his attention.
Dancing against a beautiful backdrop of mauve wisteria, the maiden, performed here by Bandō Tamasaburō V, changes
her kimono four times during the performance.

STAGE 5

SACRED AND CEREMONIAL

Sacred and Ceremonial Dance • Indigenous Australian Dance
Kpanlogo • Adumu

Sacred and Ceremonial Dance

The use of dance in religious ceremonies can be traced back to the ancient Egyptians. Images of people dancing are abundant in ancient Egyptian artefacts and depict dances that were performed at births, marriages, funerals and on royal occasions. Sacred dances were also performed for gods and goddesses.

Even today in some parts of the world such as Australia, India, Africa and western Asia, dancing is an expression of a belief in a deity, or a way to make a connection with supernatural powers. These dances are designed to celebrate and praise, and are often considered sacred because they are so deeply rooted in culture and history.

When sacred or spiritual dance is used as a form of worship, the dancer becomes closer to supernatural power through the act of dancing. An example of this is Sufi, a ceremony practised mainly in Turkish and Persian countries. Sufi dancers spin in circles for long periods of time, entering a trance state to feel closer to God. During the tribal dances of Africa, such as the Maasai jumping dance known as Adumu (see pages 80–81), unseen forces or spirits of animals are believed to enter the dancers as they perform, often as part of the transition of children into adulthood.

Spiritual dance can also be expressed as a performing art through the retelling of stories or myths. The purpose of these performances is to transport the viewer or audience closer to a deity or spirit world. Indian classical dances, such as Bharatanatyam and Kathak (see pages 68–69) and the Thai dance Khon (see pages 66–67), are considered divine art forms but are also wonderfully entertaining examples of dance-drama.

Indigenous Australian dances (see pages 76–77) are of both sacred importance and performed for entertainment. Some dances tell tales of the time of creation, known by the Aboriginal people as the Dreaming. As is the case for so many endangered cultures, dancing is a way to ensure traditions and beliefs are kept alive and passed on to younger generations.

Now Showing

A Sufi dancer takes part in a ceremony | Galata Mevlevi Lodge Museum (Whirling Dervish Hall), Istanbul, 2018

An 800-year-old tradition rooted in Islamic history, Sufi dances are considered a form of meditation through dance and can last for many hours. Dancers dressed in camel hair hats known as sikke and traditional white robes with full skirts spin in circles for long periods. The aim is for the dancers to abandon the ego by focussing on the music, on God and on the physical challenge of continuous turning. This gives them the nickname 'whirlers'. Every movement is symbolic. For example, when the right hand is positioned above and the left is below, this gesture represents taking whatever God gives and handing it out to the people.

Indigenous Australian Dance

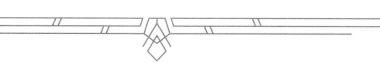

Some dances included in this book go back centuries, but for the First Peoples of Australia, their dances celebrate, and are a connection with, ancestors that existed millions of years ago. For the Aboriginal people, the relationship with each other, their history, the land, plants and animals are central to their belief systems. Aboriginal philosophy is known as the Dreaming or Dreamtime and is a way of seeing the world and time as one: past, present and future. Their dances are a way of connecting to their ancestors and passing on the beliefs that hold their communities together. Each group or tribe therefore has different customs when it comes to performing.

Storytelling plays a very important role in Indigenous Australian dances, and dancers often enact the creatures they share their home with. The Crane Dance, for example, involves dancers imitating the birds' strutting style while searching for food in the waters around

them. Other dances are part of coming-of-age ceremonies for teenagers, or are performed to incorporate tradition into a wedding or funeral service.

As part of their preparations, dancers often apply ochre (a natural clay) as body paint. Sourced from the land, ochre holds great importance for Indigenous Australians and the designs used – from dots and dashes to handprints – link back to their ancestor spirits. Dancers also wear costumes made of fur, feathers and dyed cloths.

The accompanying music is mostly vocal chanting and singing, played alongside the rhythm of wooden clapping sticks and the drone of a didgeridoo, a long tubular instrument that is blown into using circular breathing techniques.

Indigenous dance styles have made it to theatres around the world through the work of companies like Bangarra. The contemporary dance company uses Indigenous dance styles and stories to promote awareness and understanding of the persecution, prejudice and hardship First Nations have experienced in Australia. Their aim is to use art to educate, heal and bring about social change.

▷ Now Showing ◁

Yugambeh warriors dance during an Aboriginal culture show | Gold Coast, Queensland, 2016

Queensland's Aboriginal and Torres Strait Islanders enjoy sharing their culture with travellers through art galleries, festivals, walks, tours and dance shows. The Yugambeh believe the spirits of wounded warriors live in their mountains and make themselves known through scars on the mountainside and thunderstorms.

Kpanlogo

Often referred to as the soul of Africa, dance has been at the heart of African culture since Ancient Egyptians carved images of people dancing into cave walls. Unlike most Western performing traditions, it is impossible to separate dance from the other disciplines of music and storytelling within the African continent. More than a routine, dance in Africa forms a big part of everyday life.

Not many dance styles can be said to have their origin in the independence of a country, but kpanlogo is exactly that. A combined music and dance tradition and an offshoot from other recreational dances of the Ga ethnic group, kpanlogo came to prominence in the 1960s in and around Accra, the capital of Ghana. It grew as part of an urban youth movement to celebrate Ghanaian independence. In the coastal regions around Ghana, kpanlogo was also performed on Tuesdays (considered a spiritual holiday), and while today it is performed recreationally, it still takes place to celebrate all manner of occasions, from naming ceremonies to funerals, festivals and political rallies.

As with all African dance styles, the music cannot be separated from the dance; the name kpanlogo is also the name of the drums that provide the driving beat. The drums are accompanied by two other time-keeping instruments – the hand bell, or *gankogui*, and the gourd rattle, or *fou*.

An infectious dance of joy and freedom, kpanlogo is danced in pairs or in groups. The knees are bent and there is a lot of looseness in the hips, resulting in a swaying movement with accompanying gestures of the arms and hands. The dancers perform in unison, with an individual dancer coming forward now and again to take the spotlight.

At first some of the movements in kpanlogo were seen as risqué and it was almost banned by the government. But a new version which allowed more space between the dancers was eventually approved by Ghana's first president in 1965, and it has been a hugely popular and constantly evolving style of music and dance ever since.

NOW SHOWING

1: Gourd rattle (*fou*)
This bulb-shaped instrument is made from the dried vegetable of the same name.

2: Kpanlogo (*tswreshi*)
This barrel-shaped drum is usually played with two hands, and always as part of an ensemble.

3: Dancers
Two men perform kpanlogo in the Ga-Mashie district of Accra.

4: Hand bell (*gankogui*)
This instrument is made of two conical bells – the larger bell producing a lower pitch than the smaller. A wooden dowel is used as a beater.

78

Adumu

The Maasai people are an ethnic group from Kenya and Northern Tanzania. The impact of colonialism in the 18th and 19th centuries meant that many African tribal traditions were lost, but the Maasai have maintained their traditional life which revolves around rearing large herds of cattle and goats. Dance plays a big part in Maasai culture and warriors often perform special dances known as the 'adumu' – or the Maasai jumping dance.

The adumu is part of the long-observed ceremony, Eunoto, a coming-of-age ritual that takes place every generation, so around every 20 years. It includes 10 days of singing and dancing, a parade and other traditions.

The adumu is essentially a dance-off. Young warriors, known as morani, show off their prowess and strength to other members of the tribe by attempting to jump higher than their competitors. To the accompaniment of chanting, the morani enter the centre of the circle one at a time and literally jump as high and as straight as they can to the rhythm, their heels never touching the earth. The watching warriors match the pitch and volume of their voices to the height of the leaps, humming, chanting and calling loudly. The warriors' parents also sing about the courage of their children, while others sing and chant to encourage their favourite warrior.

The warriors are not permitted to use their arms as propulsion, and this is ensured by wrapping themselves in patterned cloths, known as shuka. The dancers also wear colourful beadwork necklaces and bangles, head decorations, and sometimes red ochre is painted on their faces.

After the ceremony, the morani shave their long hair as a sign of their new position as men. They are now considered to be 'senior warriors' and are free to marry and start their own families.

Now Showing

A group of young Maasai men taking part in the traditional Adumu dance
Ngorongoro Conservation Area in the Crater Highlands area of Tanzania, Eastern Africa, 2013

The robes of the morani are often made from red cloth. This vibrant colour is thought to frighten off wild animals, including lions and other big cats, which are a threat to the livestock the Maasai keep. Hunting spears are allowed to be carried during the adumu, but they are not allowed to be used for extra propulsion!

STAGE 6

SOCIAL

Social Dance • Ballroom • Viennese Waltz
Salsa • Tango • Disco • Hip Hop

Social Dance

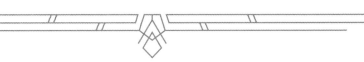

During the 16th century, European royalty regularly competed to stage increasingly lavish balls. These 'court' dances inspired the formal social dances that became popular in the 17th and 18th centuries, such as the quadrille. The waltz (see pages 88–89) then became popular in the mid 1800s and is the most famous example of the new type of 'close encounter' dance. While these dances still involved dancing with a partner, they had simplified and sometimes more risqué moves. The gradual shift to a less formal style of social dancing had begun.

By the early 20th century, young dancers were tired of mimicking the court dances of their grandparents' era. They were taking to the dance floor, often to find a soulmate, but equally to have fun. Steps were passed on between people, not via formal training, and settings gradually changed from decadent parlours to local town halls. Social dances became the place (if not the *only* place) where young people could meet potential partners and show off their moves.

Swing dance burst onto the scene in America in the late 1920s. Charleston has a long and interesting history with its origins based in Africa and, while the steps were laid down in South Carolina, the dance spread worldwide during the ragtime jazz era. Lindy Hop was perhaps the most popular swing dance, however. Created by teenagers in Harlem, New York, Lindy Hop included Charleston steps but was danced to the swing jazz of the time.

The birth of rock 'n' roll in the 1950s provided the perfect soundtrack to shift towards more rebellious moves. Disco (see pages 94–95) then emerged in the 1970s and, though less intimate than the social dances that came before, it provided the perfect way to bring people together.

The popularity of these dances spread across the globe, and today it is possible to learn and enjoy these in any city, large or small.

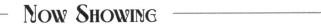

Now Showing

Dancers performing the Lindy Hop | Savoy Ballroom, Harlem, New York, 1937

The joyful spirit of Lindy Hop dancing is as infectious as the swing music it is synonymous with. Energetic and playful, improvisation is key to Lindy Hop performances. This is clearly demonstrated in 'air steps' – where a performer is literally thrown into the air by their partner! The legendary Savoy Ballroom, known as the 'Home of Happy Feet', was such a popular spot with dancers, its wooden floorboards were replaced every three years.

Ballroom

Made popular by reality TV shows such as *Strictly Come Dancing* and *Dancing With the Stars*, the glittering, glamorous, glorious world of ballroom dancing has captured the hearts of audiences around the world.

At its widest definition, ballroom dancing can be considered any type of partnered dance, but there are two main categories of competitive dances: Standard (or Smooth) and Latin.

Standard dances such as the waltz, foxtrot and quickstep originate from the European court dances such as the minuet and the quadrille. It wasn't until the early 20th century, however, that ballroom dances became specific codified dances that could be taught to the public. Husband-and-wife team Vernon and Irene Castle were key to this transformation, appearing on Broadway and in silent films, helping to make modern dancing popular again.

Standard ballroom dances tend to use the whole of the ballroom floor, with couples adopting the formal positions (referred to as 'being in hold') and circling the perimeter to the thrill and joy of the spectators. Ballroom music needs to match the dance, so instrumentals or ballads are used for the waltz, while the foxtrot and quickstep require something more jazzy.

Latin dance, which includes dances such as the paso doble, salsa and mamba, has a rich and complicated history. Its roots lie in South American culture, but with African and European influences.

The dance moves in the Latin section can be quite wild and passionate, particularly in dances like the rumba where movements are deliberately dramatic and provocative. There is more room for improvisation and new choreography, and these dances are now often performed to a soundtrack of pop or rock music that retains the Latin beat.

Now Showing

1: Standard ballroom suit

2: Standard ballroom dress

3: Latin ballroom suit
Ballroom suits are often more flamboyant than the standard, consisting of tighter trousers and low-cut shirts.

4: Latin ballroom dress
Latin ballroom costumes are more risqué than the standard. Dancers often wear revealing dresses covered in shimmering sequins.

5: Ballroom shoes
The shoes worn by male and female dancers need to be as comfortable as possible and to allow for minimal friction, ensuring the performers can glide smoothly around the dance floor. For this reason the soles are usually made of suede.
a) **Standard shoes**
b) **Latin flared heels**

1

2

3

4

5a

5b

Viennese Waltz

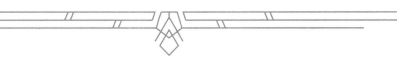

During the 19th century, Vienna was the cultural capital of central Europe. The Viennese waltz had become a craze and the many grand ballrooms of the city were filled every night with the swirling gowns of Viennese high society.

The Viennese waltz was one of the first couple dances where partners would face each other in a more intimate manner than previously seen in other court dances. At the time, this intimacy caused quite a stir, and was perceived as a decline in moral values. But the beauty of the waltz, with its graceful sweeps, was too enchanting to be dismissed. Pairs of dancers would circle the ballroom floor in the same rotation, sometimes many hundreds at once. At the same time, each couple would be constantly turning – step, slide, step footwork mirroring the 3/4 rhythm of the music, creating a mesmerising motion. Unlike the English waltz, the Viennese waltz is fast-paced, and so the long gowns were held up to avoid tripping, forming a kind of cloak, wrapped around the dancing couple.

The music became as recognised as the dance style itself, and is still played in concert halls around the world as well as an accompaniment to ballroom competitions. Austrian composer Johann Strauss II (1825–1899) composed more than 150 waltzes, including the famous *The Blue Danube*. Considered by many as the quintessential waltz, it is also acknowledged as the second national anthem of Austria.

The waltz itself has remained hugely popular. Its simplicity and rhythm makes it one of the first dances that beginners learn and it's a stalwart of the television ballroom competitions.

Now Showing

Couples take part in the Viennese waltz | Apollo Hall, Vienna, 1800s

The beautiful Apollo Hall became the centre of the Viennese waltz craze. Its grand ballrooms with high ceilings, chandeliers and ornate cornices could hold hundreds of dancers at once. At one end of the room, a full orchestra played, propelling the dancers with the latest composition by Johann Strauss II.

Salsa

The word salsa means 'sauce' in Spanish, and just like the spicy mix of ingredients, this sassy dance with its blend of different influences came to be known by the same name. In fact, 'salsa!' was often cried by musicians during their performances, spurring the performers to spice up their act.

Both in food and dance, there is no such thing as a 'pure form', and salsa is a good example of this. Based on Afro-Cuban music but with a lot of other influences, salsa has its roots in son cubano – a music style and dance that became popular in eastern Cuba in the 19th century. The music spread to Havana and then on to Latin America, eventually arriving in New York City in the 1940s. Here, Afro-Cuban music combined with Latin American elements of mambo and rumba mixed with American swing and tap, and salsa was born. By the 1970s, salsa had been embraced by the Latin American community and was hugely popular.

The rhythm is the driving force of the dance, and the music is so infectious it is hard not to dance to it! Salsa dance consists of three steps to four beats. Disrupting the regular musical pattern by emphasising the offbeats (this is called syncopation) adds character and excitement to the music. This is felt in the whole body, so while the steps are important, the looseness is reflected in the hips and shoulders as much as the feet.

Salsa is absolutely a couple dance, and interaction and fluidity are essential for any successful partnership. There is plenty of room for improvisation, but both dancers must be completely in sync to know what move is coming next!

Now a worldwide phenomenon, salsa is enjoyed in clubs, bars and festivals in almost every town or city in the world, and it is also a thriving competitive dance form, with many international competitions taking place each year. It remains a heady mix of ingredients with different styles embraced in different places.

NOW SHOWING

Two dancers hit the dance floor | Club 1830, Havana, 2010s

Fun and energetic, one of salsa's most defining features are spins. They can range from beginner spins to multiple twists at dizzying speeds!

Tango

Celebrated for its fire and passion, tango is a sensual partnered dance. With a fascinating history and a highly improvised nature, it is one of the world's most famous dances, often performed to the distinct sound of the bandoneón.

Those from Uruguay would argue that tango originated there, but Argentinians would disagree and claim theirs as the country of origin! The truth is somewhere in between. The Rio de La Plata forms a natural border between the two countries and, around 1880, was the site of mass migration. Europeans flocked to the area in search of better prospects, and there met with African and South American communities. Poor and homesick, the largely male communities traded their songs and dances. Tango was the eventual result. At the time, the dance was considered immoral and the gatherings were banned by the authorities.

Despite initial condemnation, the dance was later adopted by high society who introduced it to Paris around 1908. It proved so popular there that the years 1912–1914 became known as 'Tangomania'! As a result, the dance then quickly spread throughout the world.

Tango can be recognised by its sharp, staccato movements, head snaps and passionate attitude. Male dancers traditionally led the dance, guiding their partner in their direction of choice but today, many women lead and often men and women dance with their own gender. The constant embrace between partners historically gave tango a reputation of being slightly sinful, but there is an understanding between dancers that the intimacy remains only as long as the dance does.

Today, there are many different versions of the original tango, but they all share the same sensuality. The milongas, or dance clubs, of Buenos Aires still showcase the true spirit of authentic tango. Some are informal gatherings perfect for beginners, while others are a chance for experts to show off their skills.

Now Showing

Two dancers perform Argentine tango | Streets of Montevideo, Uruguay, 2000s

The dance of the leader and follower, tango is an intimate partnered dance that relies on communication, instinct and trust. The performers are often in close embrace, and characteristic moves include the *barrida* (sweep), *arrastre* (drag) and plenty of flourishes including leg wraps and back kicks.

Disco

Disco music emerged from the 'Philadelphia Sound' scene of the 1960s and 70s, combining both African American and Latin American influences. It became a sanctuary from all the social ills of the time, especially in New York, which was experiencing increased gang violence, soaring crime and unemployment. The now legendary clubs where disco thrived, such as The Loft and The Gallery, also provided safe and inclusive places for queer and Black communities to dance together.

While disco continued to increase in popularity during the 1970s, it was the release of the film *Saturday Night Fever* in 1977 that brought the dance style to the mainstream. Based on the life and tribulations of a young man who finds excitement and solace at the weekends in the discotheques of Brooklyn, the film included all things now synonymous with disco – flared trousers, open neck shirts, spinning coloured lights, glitter balls – all set to the disco rhythms and high falsettos of the Bee Gees.

Disco is essentially a solo activity – a much freer individual dance than other social dances – and although particular styles and routines have emerged, such as the 'Bump', the 'Hustle' and 'Voguing', disco is about making up your own movements. It is a great leveller – anyone can join in without prior practice, knowledge or even natural rhythm! The other main feature of disco – implied in the name – is that the music is not live but provided by a disc jockey (or DJ) who plays records on a turntable, usually above the dance floor.

The heyday of disco was in New York in the 1970s and 80s. Alongside this new type of social dance, a whole music scene emerged. Artists such as Donna Summer, Gloria Gaynor, Chic, and Earth, Wind and Fire gained massive popularity. Disco clubs like Studio 54 in Manhattan drew the rich and famous, who strutted their stuff on the dance floor.

Disco's legacy lives on. It is still the social dance that most people take part in, but it has also merged into many different styles of dance; it influenced the development of hip hop (see pages 96–97) and led directly to the house music and club culture of the 1980s and 1990s.

Now Showing

Revellers in action | Studio 54, New York, 1970s

Studio 54 was at the centre of the popularity of disco in the late 1970s. The club operated a strict door policy where only the coolest and most glamorous guests were allowed entry. Artists such as Andy Warhol and Salvador Dalí mixed with rock stars including David Bowie, Debbie Harry and Michael Jackson, even dancing in the presence of the actress Bianca Jagger, who allegedly arrived on a white horse!

Hip Hop

In the late 1970s, a new genre of dance started to appear on the streets and subways of New York. Driven by the hip hop music that was also emerging at that time, the dancers drew on many influences: the moves of singer James Brown, tap dance, Lindy Hop and salsa. Early crews such as The Rock Steady Crew set up sound blasters on the streets to entertain passers-by. The atmosphere became more competitive as groups challenged each other to become ever more athletic, but dancers also learned from their contemporaries, passing on skills and, most importantly, always creating new movements that they could call their own.

The movement started modestly in the Bronx in 1973 at an event organised by a young model and promoter Cindy Campbell. Aimed at young children as a 'back to school' party, the event was held in a recreation room in a local residential building, and encouraged youth away from gang membership which was dominating the local community.

At that party, Campbell's brother DJ Kool Herc (born 1955) began sampling breaks (or drum loops) from soul and funk records, and played them over and over again. Herc isolated the beats to create breaks in the music, and used two turntables to mash together

percussive sounds with popular songs. Known as breakbeat deejaying, the 'breaks' in the music gave dancers a chance to show off their moves. The dance beat which evolved encouraged a stop-start style of dance that was high energy.

Soon, other hip hop styles emerged, particularly on the West coast of America, with crews such as the Electric Boogaloos creating new techniques known as popping and locking.

By the 1980s and 90s, hip hop dance gained widespread popularity, driven by the music videos of many popular artists. Its influence on not only other modern dance styles, but also fashion, visual art and popular culture, has been immeasurable.

Now Showing

1: Breaking
Breaking performers are commonly known and b-boys or b-girls (the 'b' is for 'break'). The style is athletic and is made up of four main sections – toprock, focussing on complex footwork patterns; downrock, where dancers use their hands and feet on the ground; power moves (head spins, windmills and somersaults) which require incredible

stamina and momentum; and finally the 'freeze' where a b-dancer pauses and holds one position.

2: Popping
A dancer who is popping is much more upright – contracting and relaxing their upper body, causing a jerking movement that matches or 'hits' on the beat of the accompanying music. This gives the

impression of moving like a robot.

3: Locking
Similarly to popping, the dancer uses a freeze moment alongside a musical rhythm, but the freeze is held for much longer and the body is looser. Hand and arm movements form an important part of locking, with much wrist twirling, punching and pointing to either side.

STAGE 7

POPULAR

Popular Styles • Tap • Fred Astaire
Movie Dances • West Side Story

Popular Styles

Sometimes a dance style catches the imagination more than any other and becomes universally recognised and practised – it becomes popular! This section looks at some of those dances that have gone beyond the reach of theatres and dance studios.

Long before social media, dance crazes found a way of travelling around the world at lightning speed. Many of these styles were promoted through word of mouth, but the rise of film and television from the 1930s onwards contributed to an explosion of new dances that everyone was dying to try out. From Britain to Brazil, people took part in 'fads' such as the Twist, the Mashed Potato, the Macarena, the YMCA and countless others, and later whole routines.

Many popular styles were promoted through film and television. Bhangra, the Indian folk dance (see page 53), for example, was an integral part of the Bollywood film industry. Similarly, the popularity of tap dancing (see pages 102–103) was attributed to the rip-roaring performances of Fred Astaire and Ginger Rogers, consequently shooting the duo to stardom. Other popular styles came through the route of live musical theatre, with the success of shows like *42nd Street* and *Singin' in The Rain*.

Many of these films and musicals have become successful because of the dance elements within them, expressing the joy, energy and exuberance that only dance can. *West Side Story* (1961) and *Saturday Night Fever* (1977) would not be the iconic films that they are today without the tremendous dance scenes that are at the heart of them.

Music videos by the world's biggest superstars and social media platforms continue to give rise to new trends, including dancehall, capable of reaching audiences around the world in just a few clicks.

Now Showing

A dancehall dancer at a street party in Kingston, Jamaica, 2000s

After the initial mainstream success of the music style in native Jamaica during the 1970s and 80s, the associated dance travelled around the world. Dancehall, with sexual overtones and close interaction, is especially popular in youth culture. It is a high-attitude, high-energy dance, often replicated in many famous music videos, including those by artists Rhianna and Drake.

Tap

Nothing quite conveys the feeling of elation like tap dance. Loose and free-swinging, it is filled with humour and fun. Tap dancers are as much musicians as they are dancers; shoes fitted with heel and toe taps enable them to tap out rhythms and improvise beats by striking the floor. These cheerful performances, however, could not be further removed from the origins in which tap started.

In the United States in the early 19th century, during the time of the slave trade, enslaved people were unable to express their own traditions and so found ways of making percussion using their bodies. African American dances such as the 'patting juba', which involved hand clapping and foot stomping, combined with dances from other ethnic groups, such as the Irish jig and English clog dance.

Initially a concealed art form, tapping gained popularity after the American Civil War (1861–1865). Still undergoing extreme prejudice, African Americans were finally allowed to perform in competitions, often as part of minstrel groups (troupes of white entertainers who sang and danced while wearing black makeup alongside Black performers).

Vaudeville eventually followed – a form of light entertainment which featured singers, dancers, magicians, acrobats and actors. It was here that dancers such as Bill 'Bojangles' Robinson learned to become stars of stage and screen, paving the way for African Americans to become more widely accepted as part of mainstream entertainment.

Tap dancing numbers soon became a main feature of film and in musicals, and later spawned stars including Fred Astaire (see pages 104–105), Ginger Rogers and Gene Kelly, who mixed elements of ballroom and jazz into their routines.

Despite having fallen out of fashion, more recent films have prompted a revival, such as Oscar-winning *La La Land* (2016). Meanwhile, the work of dancers such as Savion Glover (who also choreographed the animated hit *Happy Feet* (2006) about a tap-dancing penguin!) and Ayodele Casel continue to introduce the magic of tap to new audiences.

 **Now Showing**

The Nicholas Brothers star in *Sun Valley Serenade* released 21 August 1941, USA
Directed by H. Bruce Humberstone

Fayard Antonio Nicholas (1914–2006) and his brother Harold Lloyd Nicholas (1921–2000) are considered one of the greatest tap dance acts of all time. The brothers flew through acrobatic feats so astounding that projectionists often had to rewind films and replay their dazzling dance routines for audiences who simply could not believe what they were seeing. The brothers developed a high-powered style of dance known as 'classical tap' – a combination of jazz dance, ballet, acrobatics and tap dancing.

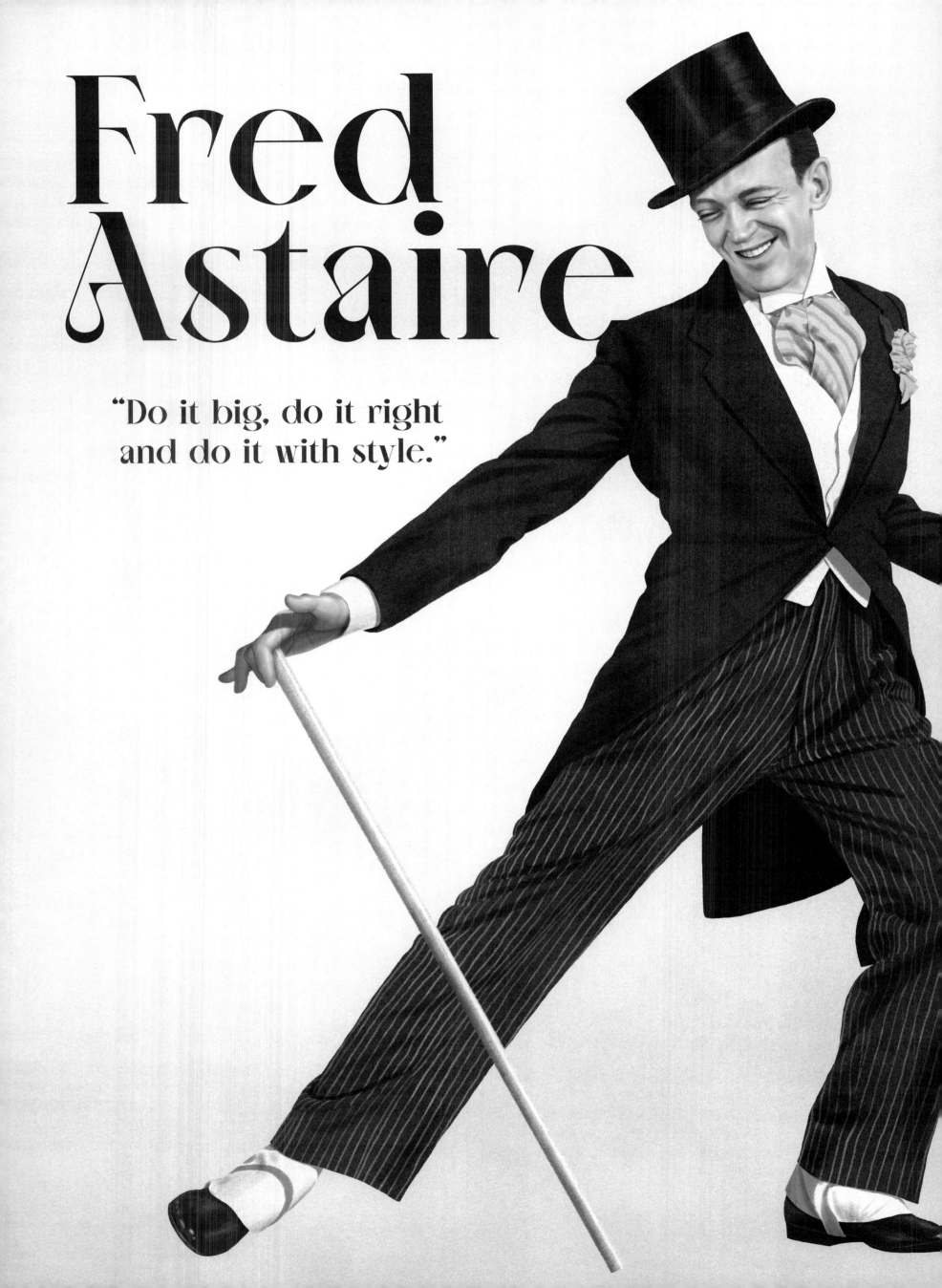

Fred Astaire

"Do it big, do it right
and do it with style."

In every dance genre, there are some performers who stand out for their elegance, style and total mastery of their craft. In tap, this person is Fred Astaire (1899–1987). A master of rhythm and the most charming of performers, Astaire could show a range of emotion in a dance from light-hearted and comical to the deepest romance. He was also a great innovator and helped develop the new 'Broadway' style of tap and ballroom.

Born Frederick Austerlitz in Omaha, USA, Astaire joined his sister in taking dance lessons at the age of four. The siblings' talent was instantly clear, and the family moved to New York so they could pursue a career in vaudeville. Their partnership made them stars and they appeared together on both stage and screen.

When his sister Adele married and took early retirement, Astaire had to find another partner. He was introduced to Ginger Rogers (1911–1995) in 1929, and a world-famous partnership was born. Their first production together in *Flying Down to Rio* (1933) was a phenomenal success, with Rogers and Astaire overshadowing the main cast members. Completely in tune rhythmically, moving in total sympathy with each other, the duo conveyed a wonderful on-screen chemistry and went on to star in another nine films together, many of them romantic.

Major dance moments in Astaire's film career include the famous 'Putting on the Ritz' from the film *Blue Skies* (1946) where his solo lobby dance turns seamlessly into a chorus of his top hat and tailed clones. In 'Dancing on the Ceiling' from the film *Royal Wedding* (1951), Astaire seems to defy gravity as he moves from dancing on the floor to the wall and then the ceiling (the room was fitted onto a giant contraption that allowed it to turn in front of the camera).

Remarkably, Astaire often insisted that complete dance routines were filmed in one take and not edited afterwards. This reinforces the amazing concentration and stamina involved in executing these complex routines, and cements Astaire's place in history as a national and international icon.

Now Showing

Fred Astaire stars in *Blue Skies* released 16 October 1946, USA | Directed by Stuart Heisler

Famously known as Astaire's 'last dance' (he announced his retirement during the production of the film), 'Puttin' on the Ritz' (written by Irving Berlin, 1888–1989) provided the soundtrack to one of the most imaginative and memorable dance routines of Astaire's career. The solo tap performance featured a routine using a cane, as had become synonymous with Astaire, and the final section featured no less than nine Astaires, all dancing in unison.

Movie Dances

Since the invention of cinema, many people have fallen in love with dance through the screen rather than the stage. From early Hollywood musicals such as *Top Hat* (1935) through to *La La Land* (2016), dance has been used as an essential aspect of storytelling in film.

The first dance film was made in 1894 – a short production by Thomas Edison of the dancer Ruth Dennis creating beautiful butterfly-inspired movements with her skirt. Initially, dance movies lacked any kind of plot, but when sound was introduced in 1929, dance could be put to music and therefore become part of a plot. This advance in technology coincided not only with the Golden Age of Hollywood but also the Great Depression (1929–1939), resulting in a demand for feel-good movies.

Director Busby Berkeley (1895–1976) stood out for his spectacular choreography and lavish sets. Uniquely, Berkeley's productions were often filmed from above, giving the illusion of a kaleidoscope, but were in fact made up of hundreds of dancers performing in perfect unison. These dazzling performances which were later replicated in many films and animations, including Disney's *The Lion King* (1994) scene 'I Just Can't Wait to be King'. Ballroom dance and tap were commonplace in movies by the 1930s, with Fred Astaire (see pages 104–105) and child actress Shirley Temple gradually phasing out Berkeley's reign. This introduced a new era of dance in film – musicals – and the 1940s and 50s were filled with iconic productions including *Singin' in the Rain* (1952).

Later, the music itself, whether rock or disco, inspired films such as *Grease* (1978), *Fame* (1980) and *Flashdance* (1983). Other films put dance at the centre of the story, notably the multi award-winning *Billy Elliot* (2000), featuring the tale of a boy from North East England who took up ballet despite the stigma. The film went on to encourage a whole generation of male ballet dancers.

Whether the classic 'Time Warp' featured in the cult film *The Rocky Horror Picture Show* (1975) or the mass Bollywood dance scene in *Slumdog Millionaire* (2008), the phenomena of dance in film looks set to thrill cinema audiences for a long time to come.

Now Showing

Patrick Swayze and Jennifer Grey star in *Dirty Dancing* released 21 August 1987, USA
Directed by Emile Ardolino

Starring Patrick Swayze and Jennifer Grey, *Dirty Dancing* is perhaps considered the most cult dance movie of all time. The duo create the perfect on-screen romance, as Grey's character 'Baby' falls in love with dance instructor Johnny Castle while on holiday. Sensual and emotionally charged, the most memorable – and, incredibly, unrehearsed – scene of the film is undoubtedly 'The Lift'. Requiring unwavering bravery, stamina and strength, Baby runs full pelt into Castle's arms before being lifted into the air.

West Side Story

One of the most important musicals in American history, *West Side Story* burst onto Broadway in 1957 with its unflinching depiction of social struggle. A far cry from the glamorous and upbeat performances popular at the time, *West Side Story*, with its hot-blooded dance routines and gritty songs, represented a turning point in musical theatre.

Set in post-Second World War New York, the story is a contemporary adaptation of William Shakespeare's *Romeo and Juliet*, based on the real struggles and social unrest faced by migrants living in the city at that time. At the centre of the story are two rival teenage gangs – the Jets (European migrants) and the Sharks (of Puerto Rican heritage) – who continually fight over territory.

Themes of racism, poverty and violence are conveyed via moving choreography. Audiences, however, were shocked and appalled upon its initial release in the 1950s: the fact that three characters are killed off was completely unexpected and went against the usual subject matter of musicals. Yet there are also tender and heart-breaking moments between the musical's main stars Maria and Tony – two lovers on opposing sides – and audiences were drawn to the story despite the violence.

The success of the musical lies not only in its ability to reflect the social struggles of the day, but in its mastery of portraying the spirit, tenacity and optimism of the young people behind these issues. Jerome Robbins' (1918–1998) choreography of the two rival gangs is masterful, depicting swagger and athleticism in both classical and popular dance styles. Graceful ballet combines with snappy jazz to exude the coolness of these teenagers in unexpected ways.

The Broadway show ran for more than 700 performances, making it a smash hit. The film adaptation in 1961 was also hugely popular and won ten Oscars in 1962 making it the musical film with the most academy awards to this day. In 2021, the beloved storyline hit screens once again, this time directed by Hollywood royalty Steven Spielberg (born 1946) and featuring a more diverse cast than its original incarnation.

▷——————————— Now Showing ———————————◁

**Scenes from the *West Side Story* musical, premiered 26 September 1957 at Winter Garden Theatre, New York
Directed and choreographed by Robert Wise and Jerome Robbins | Music by Leonard Bernstein**

Premiered on Broadway, the award-winning musical was created by Robbins, Bernstein (1918–1990), the composer Stephen Sondheim (1930–2021) and playwright Arthur Laurents (1917–2011). All four contributed to the whole production but it is perhaps the music and choreography that made this the masterpiece that it is. Both Robbins and Bernstein had one foot in the classical world and the other in the worlds of cha-cha and mambo. This can particularly be seen in the gang fight scene, which features a mixture of ballet and cha-cha moves.

Index